SCM STUDYGUIDE TO CH

SCM STUDYGUIDE TO CHURCH LEADERSHIP

Jon Coutts

scm press

© Jon Coutts 2019

Published in 2019 by SCM Press
Editorial office
3rd Floor, Invicta House,
108–114 Golden Lane,
London EC1Y 0TG, UK
www.scmpress.co.uk

SCM Press is an imprint of Hymns Ancient & Modern Ltd (a registered charity)

Hymns Ancient & Modern® is a registered trademark of
Hymns Ancient & Modern Ltd
13A Hellesdon Park Road, Norwich,
Norfolk NR6 5DR, UK

Scripture quotations are from the New Revised Standard Version of the Bible, Anglicized
Edition, copyright © 1989, 1995 by the Division of Christian Education of the National
Council of the Churches of Christ in the USA. Used by permission. All rights reserved.

British Library Cataloguing in Publication data

A catalogue record for this book is available
from the British Library

978 0 334 05778 9

Typeset by Regent Typesetting Ltd
Printed and bound by
Ashford Colour Press

Contents

Part 4 Meetings

Tables

Preface

In some ways, it is a great time to be a church leader. Leadership resources are everywhere, offering to help make us visionaries, strategists, facilitators, cheerleaders, champions, empowerers, team-builders, managers, or all of the above. Whatever kind of leader you want to be, there is a book for that, if not a podcast and network as well. The cumulative effect is this feeling that if only you could just do this or that you would unleash the potential in yourself and your church. At times it is inspiring; other times overwhelming. Unfortunately, whatever sort of leader you are, chances are there are people who would like you to be something else, and there are all those resources out there to affirm their expectations.

Due to the plurality of leadership experiences in our lives we should not be surprised if we have a variety of feelings about *leading*, let alone *being led*. A past experience of authoritarian leadership might cause us to balk at all of it, annoyance at meddling middle-managers might send us running for cover, or a predilection towards autonomy might lean us towards those leaders who leave us well enough alone. On the other hand, many of us will be able to think of a leader without whose positive influence we would not be who we are today; a leader we want to be like one day. Put it all together and maybe a studyguide to church leadership is not such a bad idea.

What are we even talking about when we talk about leadership? Is it the catch-all term for anything that bears a family resemblance to organizational roles like management or government, or to churchly roles like preaching or pastoring? Or is leadership an intangible thing, like influence or persuasion? Perhaps resources are so ubiquitous because leadership is an umbrella-term, under which huddle managers and recruiters, speakers and coaches, authorities and activists alike. One might think the qualifier *church* narrows the leadership options, but because of its intrinsic diversity it arguably widens the umbrella.

Some may celebrate this open-endedness and feel the fewer parameters the better. Church is a place to be creative and collaborative. In that case the notion of *theology for church leadership* might feel like the terms and conditions for using software. Scroll down and click *okay* and be done with it. You see this when someone says we need to focus less on doctrine and more on what happens 'on the ground'; less on the structures and more on the Spirit; less on preparation and more on the movement of God. The suggestion is that these pairings are opposed, which is itself a notion that tends to go unexplored. But there is nothing quite so theological as the claim to not need theology. If we ignore theology we should not presume that our church leadership will have much to do with the Christian God. Christianity is based on the belief that Jesus Christ is true God and true human, and that Jesus is God's communication with us. Divinity has had words with humanity, and has asked us to pass it on. To believe this is to accept the call to communicate God in word and deed together by the grace of God in the power of the Spirit. Our very flourishing as a church requires that we heed this God together, by grace following faithfully rather than carrying along on our own.

We might be excused, of course, if we have a negative gut reaction to the complexities and technicalities of doctrine and biblical study. One encounter with arid dogmatics or thick encyclopaedias of biblical criticism can be enough to send some of us headlong into a lifetime preference for devotional literature and intuitive prayer, leaving the academic disciplines to the scholars. At best this can be reckoned an important distribution of the gifts and ministries of the church, which God works together for good among those who love and serve the Lord. At worst this is a siloing off of church from academy, practitioners from scholars – which leads inadvertently to a separation of theology from the life of the church. But if Jesus is God with us, then church is where we resist the idea that never the twain shall meet. Rather than seeing practicality and theology as opposing poles, we need to resist the false dichotomy and recall that our daily bread is to heed the word of God together, to seek understanding in faith, and to share truth in love. Without holding theology and practice together we run the risk of severing hearts from minds, bodies from souls, individuals from groups, and communities from each other, plunging ourselves into the arrogance and ignorance of the daily grind of untested ideas and tasks. Church leaders have their heads and feet in both kinds of work, helping people see practice and theology reconciled in the body of Christ.

One of the worst cultural adaptations committed by the church in modern times came about from its acceptance of the secularizing idea that religion is a private affair. This was part of an important societal move toward greater tolerance, the first fruit of genuine liberation from oppression and repression. But it has run shallow, leaving us awash in different belief systems, none of us quite sure where to find meaningful common ground. The modern move has run shallow in church as well. If faith is fundamentally personal then it is easily rendered incommunicable and unaccountable not only to public life but to the shared life of the church. There may be some positives to being *spiritual but not religious*, but we should not kid ourselves that this is un-theological or irrelevant to leadership. For better or for worse, if personal encounter tops corporate communion as the focal point of Christian life and worship, then the focus of church leadership shifts towards modes of operation that maximize individual self-expression and direction. We might be okay with that, but if churches only parrot the public slogan – *whatever works for you, as long as it does not hinder somebody else* – they may be tolerant but little else.

In reality, churches organized around such a low common denominator actually tend to gather into loose demographic affiliations of personal prefer-ence, thereby contributing more to segregation than true tolerance. Turned more into collectives than communions, churches then turn to marketing and management for primary tools of leadership functionality. Biblical theology curves in on the self, now made to service the individual encounter with God that is assumed to be the centre of everything. Questions of principle are per-ceived as the obstructions of back-row curmudgeons, and the pragmatics that produce measurably effective results for the favoured demographic carry the day. Grudgingly or happily, theologians accept this state of affairs, turn into isolated intellectuals, and lose their place in the church's life together. Not only do their various disciplines get cut off from the church but also from each other, just as market forces distance popular literature from more learned tomes. Over time there is a tragic severing of the church's hands from its arms, its lobes from its ears. The body of Christ hacks away at itself and lets stereotypes and silos prevail. To make matters worse, in the middle are church leaders, torn one way or the other. Perhaps torn apart inside.

Thankfully the very thing church is about – God with us ever anew in Christ – keeps us from settling for this worst-case scenario. There is always grace for us, in faith. But faith seeks understanding, or else it becomes faith in *belief itself,* settling into the idolatry of erudite intellectualism or exalted intuition. And faith seeks communion, or else it becomes faith in *believers themselves,* driving into a cul-de-sac of private individualism or rebuilt nostalgia. Modernity may be full of departures from Christian faith – but there is always a road back with Jesus Christ. Secular individualism may tear at the fabric of Christian communion – but the Holy Spirit stitches it together afresh each day. This is the beautiful mess of reconciliation that puts church leaders right in the middle. Bureaucrats and fundamentalists may retreat into their tick-boxes, but church leaders attend to the multidimensional gospel of Emmanuel, God with us, whose saving work carries on in concrete realities of the world reconciled in Christ.

One of the most axiomatic biblical passages for church leadership is Romans 12, but it must not be read apart from the doxology that leads into it at the end of chapter 11:

> O the depth of the riches and wisdom and knowledge of God! How unsearchable his judgements and how inscrutable his ways!
>
> 'For who has known the mind of the Lord?
>
> Or who has been his counsellor?'
>
> 'Or who has given a gift to him,
>
> to receive a gift in return?'
>
> For from him and through him and to him are all things. To him be the glory forever. Amen. (Rom. 11.33–36)

This passage puts us in our place and reminds us of the depth of the mysteries of God, which are not handed over for us to manage in our own ways and to our own ends. But notice that it does not stop there. The mysteries of God are not exactly withheld from us, either. This two-sided consequence of the mystery of God often gets lost in translation, so let us be sure to take note. It is 'so that you may not claim to be wiser than you are, brothers and sisters, [that] I want you to understand this mystery' (Rom. 11.25). We are given the revelation of God, not on our own terms and to our own devices, but in a way where God remains God. God with us is how God is known by us. It is this rich theological claim that sets the transition to church life and leadership:

> I appeal to you therefore, brothers and sisters, by the mercies of God, to present your bodies as a living sacrifice, holy and pleasing to God, which is your spiritual [*logikē*] worship. (Rom. 12.1)

As if it knows nothing about our modern division of theory from practice, that Greek word *logikē* – which can also be translated 'reasonable' – seems to resist the modern tug of war between soul and mind, spirituality and study, life and theology. So it goes:

> Do not be conformed to this world, but be transformed by the renewing of your minds, so that you may discern what is the good and acceptable and perfect will of God. (Rom. 12.2, as per the footnote)

If Romans anticipates the theory/practice divide, then this exhortation seems roundly to reject it. What comes next is of vital importance to church leadership:

> For by the grace given to me I say to everyone among you not to think of yourself more highly than you ought to think, but to think with sober judge-ment, each according to the measure of faith that God has assigned. For as in one body we have many members, and not all the members have the same function, so we, who are many, are one body in Christ, and individually we are members of one another. (Rom. 12.3–5)

The passage goes on to name several graces given by God in Christ, including the gift of the leader to the church. This book is meant as a reckoning with what that means.

In its past life, what you are about to read was a series of 12 lectures for a module called 'Exploring Leadership and Theology for Ministry and Mission'. With such a bulky title and so little time, it felt like the set-up to satisfy no one. But we set out to explore the theology of church leadership with attentiveness to the Scriptures on the one hand and the current realities of ministry and mission on the other, and lo and behold, as so often happens, the more we pressed into the Word of God and basics of Christian ecclesiology the more challengingly applicable we found it to be. My hope is that this studyguide serves you in much the same way.

Before we begin, allow me therefore to express my gratitude to the (former) students of Trinity College Bristol who thoughtfully discussed some of this material with me, most especially Helen O'Sullivan, Katherine Brayford, and Tom Dove, who then read various drafts of this work and helped me to clarify and improve it considerably. I am grateful also to my faculty colleagues

– particularly Justin Stratis, Jamie Davies, and Helen Collins – with whom I have thought much of this through (and tried to learn to live it). For similar reasons I give thanks for those with whom I studied at Kings College Aberdeen, Briercrest Seminary, and Canadian Bible College (now Ambrose University). I am also hugely grateful to those among whom I have ministered in the churches of Canada and Scotland – Bob, Lorena, Barry, Cindy, Trevor, Phyllis, Linda, Ralph, Jen, Dwayne, Tasha, Colin, Clayton, Tamara, Dale, Dani, Andrew, Anne Wilma, Glenn, Carol, Kevin, Andrea, Mark, Pat, Warren, Eunice, Carla, Chris, Aaron, Micah, and Joshua – through whom the Spirit has brought much grace and truth. It is humbling to think how many more there are whom space does not permit me to name. Finally, I thank God for my lovely wife Angie and our sons Elijah, Brady, Jesse, and Mattias, who have been faithful sojourners in life and service to the church.

In what follows we will not shy away from confrontation with the illusory blueprints of the 'celebrity pastor' or the 'managerial guru' that hang over us like an oppressive standard or a furtive spotlight. But this book will not be primarily polemical. We deconstruct modern preconceptions in order to renew a con-structive vision of church leadership and to provide a matrix for appropriating contemporary wisdom *Christianly*. My hope is that this studyguide will be read-able and relevant for first-timers and long-timers both, calling us (back) to what church is about and how it proceeds, so that the shape of our creative energies will be focused and formed by that which makes church leadership Christian. As we work through 12 basic questions of church leadership with a view towards contextual application, my prayer is that rather than feeling boxed in by the never-ending inward spirals of our own devices and expectations, readers will feel freed for church leadership as they focus on making the main things the main things, and improvise from there in the daily grace of Christ.

Part 1

Ends

1

Tensions: What is So Good About Leadership?

Some people feel born to lead. Others feel physically ill at the thought. Not all of the former make for good Christian leaders, and some of the latter surprise themselves. In my youth I certainly balked at the idea of following in my father's footsteps and becoming a pastor. Some of this was from seeing the stress involved backstage, but most of it had to do with my personality. Whether from introversion or insecurity, I preferred to observe rather than be observed, to read the room before speaking up, and to follow instead of sticking my neck out to lead. It was not until my twenties that I began to consider such a thing, and only then because of a conviction I could not shake. Even with a Bible College degree, a pastoral internship, denominational licensing, commissioning as a local pastor, and ordination to permanent ministry, I still struggled to feel comfortable in my own skin as a church leader. I kept holding myself up to the standard of other personalities, and falling short. For years I thought I was the only one who felt this way, but it turns out this is actually a common story.

In my experience it is not the case that Christian leadership always comes naturally – either you have it or you do not – and upon further study I have found that this is also not true theologically. Church leadership is received, discerned, and learned, even by those who find themselves apt for it. This is why those who do not gravitate towards leadership often find God calling and gifting them for it anyway, and those who seem like 'natural leaders' often have to work against the grain of their encultured habits and premises in order to lead the particular group called *church*. We will come back to this point in due course, but before we discuss whether leadership is natural we need to back up further and ask in what sense it is even *good*.

Our initial feelings about leadership tend to be a reflection of our life experiences.

Explore this by reflecting on the following questions:

- Do you sit comfortably in the leader's seat, do you prefer the 'second chair', or do you tend to observe and follow at a pace?
- Have you experienced negligent or abusive authority in your past which left you in a position of ambivalence or even revulsion at the whole idea?
- Have you had to lead in situations that have made you wary of ever taking on such an onerous and isolating burden again?
- If you were to place your feelings about leadership on a spectrum between necessary evil, provisional good, and flourishing ideal, where would you land?
- Do you have a different answer depending whether you are leading or being led?
- Has your life experience shaped the degree to which you think leadership is good?

It is of course a theological question whether leadership is a created good, an evil impostor, or somewhere in between. Is it a God-intended part of our human flourishing or is it parasitic corruption of human equality? Is it a so-called necessary evil, an imperfect means of keeping human selfishness and competition in check? Or is it what we call a provisional good, temporarily provided by God for the preservation of sinning creatures on their way to fuller redemption? Do we envision a future in which there is no need for us to submit to leaders anymore, which is how we imagine it would have been if sin and enmity had not plunged us into conflict? These questions are not immaterial. How we answer them will go a long way to informing not just our theology of church leadership but our approach to its purposes and practicalities.

The trend in recent decades towards servant leadership and teamwork (even in organizations with clear hierarchical structures) suggests an underlying desire to downplay lines of authority and to emphasize equality and collaboration. All manner of global, socio-political, and cultural-historical stories could be told to explain this trend, and for the most part I imagine most of us would consider it a good one. Servant leadership is a positive societal development, both in and outside the church. However, there are motivational and implementational tendencies within this trend that might not be considered entirely positive. For instance, where there is a growing distrust of leadership that has even a whiff of authority to it, there is often an exacerbated self-centredness that demands everything be suited to personal specifications before submitting to a larger purpose or another's plan. History has certainly shown that there are plenty of problems with normalized social roles of submission, but is *all* submission bad? If submission is bad then so is authority, which is why so many prefer to talk about *leadership*. But it is not altogether clear that a shift from authority to leadership gets us out of this jam.

The irony of servant leadership is that the effort to avoid *authority and submission* in principle may end up submitting nobody to anyone, and the leaders to everyone. The question might then be asked whether servanthood is a *mode* of leadership, or the undermining of leadership altogether. Anyone applying to be a servant leader certainly has good reason to inquire what they might be signing themselves up for. Will they be asked to lead or to do the bidding of a select minority? Will they be held responsible for outcomes over which they had little to no authority? Will their commission to lead be scaled to their powers of people-pleasing or persuasion? I do not think it is cynical to ask such things. For all we might say about the importance of servant leadership, we might also sympathize with those who say that accepting such roles feels like walking into a trap.

What this line of thought exposes is the fact that, however we might reframe it, leadership is all tangled up with questions of authority, submission, and responsibility. I suspect it is common to be relatively comfortable submitting to authority in a work environment (the boss is the boss after all) or in civil affairs (the law is the law after all), but to see church as something of a reprieve from such arrangements. Church may be attractive precisely because it comes with no such strings attached. We can choose our churches and lend support to leaders up to the point at which they ask us to do something we did not ask them to ask us to do, making church a liberating kind of group to which to belong.

Sometimes an intolerance for authority appears most pronounced within organizations that run on the goodness of people's own hearts. It can be in church – where our motivations are often deeply personal – that we are least likely to want to submit to someone else's rationale for doing something. 'Servant leadership' can be the good face we put on it when we are subconsciously unwilling to tolerate a more directive mode of leadership. Churches touting servant leadership may be thinking less about serving where their commissioned ministers guide them, and more about insisting the clergy service a particular set of social or religious demands. At worst, church leadership can become more like customer service than Christian service, and it is not always easy to tell the difference. I do not wish to over-generalize, but I daresay most of us will *feel* these dynamics at work well before we are able to name them, let alone do anything about them.

What is so good about leadership? The question is a timely one, but is not entirely the product of our times. There is a tension here which finds precedence in the Bible itself. We might suppose that the Bible takes leadership and authority roles for granted, but the picture gets fuzzier when we take a moment to consider the following two questions:

1 When is the first time the Bible says any humans will lead other humans?
2 What does the Bible say when the people of Israel first ask for a king?

In the first case, the answer is that the first time any human is explicitly said to have any sort of 'rule' over any other human is in the context of the curse of sin. It is Genesis 3.16, wherein God says to the woman: 'Your desire will be for your husband, and he will rule over you.' If this is not the origin of human leadership, it is at least an indication of its pollution by the advent of enmity.

And if this suggests that the evolution of human leadership is tainted by the curse of sin, the suggestion is only underlined in the second case, when God responds to the Israelite request for a king. 1 Samuel 8.6–7 says not only that it 'displeased Samuel when they said, "Give us a king to govern us"' but that God said 'they have not rejected you, but they have rejected me from being king over them'. As the story goes, God provided a king and even made good on the provision, but left a hint that this was less than ideal. However we interpret all of this, we at least see the biblical precedent for starting our theology of church leadership with the question whether such a thing is in the first instance even a created good.

There is plenty of precedent for this question in the theological tradition of the church as well. Even before getting into the complexities of the Protestant Reformation, as an example we only need look at the inquiries of two of the foremost ancient church theologians who predated it. Consider the fourth-century North African bishop Augustine and the thirteenth-century friar Thomas Aquinas. To access these in a way that is true to the ancient context we need to frame the question in terms of government specifically rather than leadership generally, but when we ask if it is a created good we find that Augustine and Thomas are of two minds on the matter. The short answer is that Augustine suggested *No, this was not the original plan*, and Thomas suggested *Yes, government is a created good*. Of course, it is a bit more complicated than that.

For his part, Augustine considered the government of some humans by others to be part of God's gracious response to the Fall into sin rather than an original good of the created order as such. In book 19 chapter 15 of *City of God*, Augustine rather famously said that 'the first just men were set up as shepherds of flocks, rather than as kings of men'. This was part of an argument that the 'order of nature' in which God created us put humans in dominion over other creatures, but not necessarily over other humans (XIX.15). Augustine's understanding was that peace between human beings coincided with 'the duly ordered agreement' of each person's soul, mind, and body within the self as a consequence of peace with God. This 'mutual fellowship in God' is 'the peace of the Heavenly City' – 'a perfectly ordered and perfectly harmonious fellowship in the enjoyment of God' – and it is this 'state of peace' which has been disturbed by our sin, even as we mercifully remain within 'the scope of order' (XIX.13). Now we are 'at once social by nature and quarrelsome by perversion' (XII.28). In other words, as the first 11 chapters of Genesis show us, proper dominion has turned to domination because of the fall of pride (XVI.4), which 'hates a fellowship of equality under God, and seeks to impose its own dominion of fellow men, in place of God's rule' (XIX.12).

However, God has not withdrawn. In fact, Augustine says, 'God turns evil choices to good use' (XI.17) by graciously providing peace and order even within our structures of disorder. This is the earthly city, 'created by self-love', in which we live at the same time as we live in the heavenly city 'by love of God' (XVI.28). So for Augustine 'the heavenly city' is accessible to us by the grace of God even in the 'earthly city' of our enmity and sin, but as long as we live on this earth we are given modes of governance as a provision for our disorder (XIX.16). This is not a bad thing per se – in fact when it is ordered to the common love of God it has the potential to be a real reflection of the heavenly city on earth. But this earthly provision of peace is enacted within the circumstances of our prideful competition, which means it graciously works towards and sometimes enforces compromises (XIX.12). Those who by faith identify with the heavenly city do not abandon their neighbours in the earthly city, but like pilgrims in a foreign land they work towards and 'make use of this peace also' (XIX.17).

To come back to Genesis and 1 Samuel from an Augustinian perspective, then, we could say that Israel's choice of a king signalled a rejection of God's preferred mode of governance through prophets, but that God could still use it for good on the way to its fulfilment by Christ. We could also say that if the hierarchical relation between Adam and Eve was not a created good but an exacerbation of sin, it could still be made relatively good in the love of God, even if Christ's work would bring about something better. From this perspective, relations and roles of leadership and authority are a provisional good that can be for better or worse to the degree that they serve peace in the earthly context and are oriented to the peace of heaven by virtue of the common love and grace of Christ.

For his part, centuries later and cultures apart, Thomas Aquinas came closest to addressing our question in his *Summa Theologiae* in a discussion of the place of Law. In sections 90–97 of *Prima Secundae* (1a2ae), Thomas differs slightly from Augustine in that he sees law and order as something more than a provision for sin. For Thomas it comes back to the divine intent for human beings not to operate alone, found in Genesis 2.18, which implies an effort on our part to be 'well adjusted to the common good' (90.1–2, 92.1). One of the good things about creation – even before sin comes on the scene – is that we participate each in our own way to the very ordering of the goods of creation. This implies an ordered diversity of societal roles, including the role of governance. Laws, Thomas says, are 'proportioned to the common good' for 'all manner of personalities, occu-pations, and occasions. Many types go to make up the political community, a variety of business serves its common interest' (96.1). In this it is not 'unfair' to have 'special regard' for those who have been authorized and 'entrusted with a particular commission in the matter' (97.4).

In the view of both Augustine and Thomas, then, leadership and authority can be done for ill or for good, but there is a slight difference of opinion about what they are in principle. What Augustine might call an earthly provisional good that stands in need of heavenly fulfilment or replacement by Christ, Thomas would call a created good that is poised to be perfected by grace. What they agree on, to put it in Augustine's terms, is that if the earthly is 'perfectly ordered' to the heavenly then there is 'harmonious fellowship in the enjoyment of God' that includes an 'arrangement of things equal and unequal in a pattern which assigns each to its proper position' and may well involve 'giving and obeying orders' (XIX.13). The question, then, is what we do with that.

Does this take us back to the hierarchical organization of bygone eras, which included subordination not only of children to parents but women to men and slaves to masters, not to mention the eventual invention of racial categories and the subordination of some races to others for the alleged good of the globe? Does it lead us to a division of church from state, workplace and household, such that the Christians do the best they can within those other orders, but then turn to church to come up with the best approximation of a heavenly ordered governance they can manage? Or does it lead to a chastened view of leadership and authority, which makes the most of it outside the church, but tries to avoid it at all costs within? Churches that opt for the latter view might do so from an Augustinian aspiration to operate by heavenly-city consensus when in the fellowship of the saints, and churches that opt for the former view might do so from a Thomist belief that it is in the church that we might see law and order perfected by grace.

The New Testament appears to take leadership for granted in the church. It is not even wrong to *want* to be a church leader. 1 Timothy 3.1 says: 'The saying is sure: whoever aspires to the office of bishop [or overseer] desires a noble task.' The assumption in what follows is that the leaders of the church will follow the pattern of the surrounding culture and be drawn from the class of married men with children – but that does not strictly necessitate that such a pattern is normative for all times and places. What it does suggest is that church oversight remains a 'noble task'. Depending how we translate the Greek we might even call it a good work or a beautiful business! The question is: *what kind of good is it?*

If leadership is believed to be an outcome of (or response to) the fall then churches may tend to idealize the absence of structure, spiritualize the spontaneous and unstructured, and even go so far as to equate *intuition* with *freedom*. On the other hand, if leadership is believed to be a good and perfectible part of the original created order, then churches may tend to idealize the structures that approximate their imagined perfection, spiritualize social-historical norms and ingrained habits, and even go so far as to equate the *status quo* with *holiness*. There is more at stake here than just our *attitudes* towards leadership and structure. The very politic or group dynamic of a church will shift depending on what we think is the good of leadership and authority. This becomes clear when we move from the fourth- and thirteenth-century milieux of Augustine and Thomas to the sixteenth- and eighteenth-century movements of Reformation and Enlightenment that have shaped the modern world.

Sometimes it surprises Protestants to learn that most Reformers were not against church structure and authority as such, but were trying to get the Roman Catholic Church to face up to its abuses of power. In most cases what resulted was a shift in the *mode* of church governance, not a move away from it. The Reformers were part of a massive paradigm shift that took place in the West centuries ago, now known historically as the birth of modernity, and philosophically as 'the turn to the subject'. In short, what took root in the sixteenth century and took hold over time was a multi-faceted effort not only to restore the dignity and liberty of persons but to reorient political life as much as possible around the subjective interests of individuals. Anyone with even a cursory understanding of this historical moment will be able to think of a few social justice projects that came out of it that are worthy to be celebrated and continued: things such as the abolition of slavery, the rise in equality for women, and the reparation of race relations, to name a few. None of these large-scale movements is irrelevant to the task of church leadership (and will come up later on), but for now we take note of the change in cultural conditions that has made this a book about church *leadership* rather than *governance* (which is what it would likely have been five decades ago).

When sixteenth-century English philosopher Thomas Hobbes looked at the issue before him – in short, how to honour individual liberties and still have a stable society – he saw that the deck of human nature was stacked against success. Combining the premise that human nature is never content with what it has with the observation that the earth does not produce enough to go around, Hobbes concluded that the result of individual liberty would be an unbridled 'war of all against all'. For all that might be said about the deposition of old authorities, then, there remained a need for some kind of social contract that included the rule of authority. What differentiates this type of political thinking from that which went before it is that the society is not ordered any longer towards a unitary view of the common good (to which all should have to fall in line), but is a contract ordered towards the relative self-interest of individuals. Each individual enters into it not primarily for the common good, but primarily because it is in their self-interest to prefer the contract to outright chaos. One need not be altruistic or even agree with somebody's utopian vision for society to see that there are personal (even selfish) benefits to pursuing (or at least agreeing to) a relatively common good.

There have been manifold ways of arranging modern liberal democracies within this paradigm shift, but the fundamental impulse on which it depends is that most of us will see that it is in our own self-interest to respect the self-interest of others, and thus to contribute to such an environment by doing so. The long-story-short is that modernity is replete with attempts to philosophize about the political system and tinker with the social arrangements to make this work. Some maintain a high view of the role of authority structures, like Hobbes, and some heighten the liberty of the individual to the diminishment of government as much as possible, but most stem from that basic turn to the self on which modernity is founded.

When eighteenth-century Scottish philosopher Adam Smith looked at the same world Hobbes was describing, he argued that the way to manage self-interest towards a common good was not necessarily to limit (or govern) it but to *harness* it – and the mechanism for doing this was the marketplace. The basic idea was that healthy competition on an open market would not only serve the self-interest of choosy customers, but would also have the knock-on effect of being good for society in the long run. If we imagine the modern society as a series of mechanisms for empowering individuals to choose their own good (and by so choosing to give collective shape to the social whole), then democracy enables it with our ballots, and the market with our wallets. Whether one was privileged to have a ballot or a wallet was another story.

It probably goes without saying that this has had a significant effect on modes of government and on the means by which influence is gained and held in the modern world. The reason I relay this history here is not only because its relevance for church leadership is profound, but also because it tends to be invisible to us until we name it. Fast forward a few centuries from Hobbes and Smith and now we see that leadership revolves less around enforced authority and hinges instead on earned influence and the power of persuasion. Much of the water under the bridge in recent decades of church leadership resourcing has been coming to grips with this change one way or the other. Some are critical and resistant to it; others appear to accept it uncritically in a hurry to get on with the progressive programme. My goal is simply for us to reckon with it. To that end we conclude with the influential and poignant observations of Alasdair MacIntyre.

Reflecting in great detail on the history narrated briefly above, Alasdair MacIntyre's 1981 book *After Virtue* showed how naïve it would be to imagine that when modern Western societies did away with power-hungry emperors and philosopher kings they got rid of authorities altogether. Tracing the paradigm shift both historically and philosophically, MacIntyre explains how the move from a society ordered around institutions to a society ordered around the individual does not ultimately free us from authority figures, but renders us captive to new ones. When old authorities are deposed or diminished there is certainly an authority vacuum that opens up in society, but we are kidding ourselves if we think it is filled by the autonomous self. In actuality there are all kinds of influential powers that rush in to fill the vacuum. The rejection of old authorities over time created not an absence but a shift in powers. This might in many ways be a good thing, but the fact is that it happened relatively slowly and invisibly because it was not institutionalized, and with this there comes a problem: such invisibility carries with it a lack of accountability and intentionality that imperceptibly and even insidiously surrenders charge of the modern world. The measure of self-rule we experience in the modern world is immense compared with most ancient individuals, but to call it self-rule would be an illusion, since new authorities have flooded in to fill the gap. Even in places where old authority structures still hold, these figures are the ones who rise to power and are the leaders of the modern world; and church leaders are expected to be just like them. So who are they?

The new authority figures that run society (whether they want to do so or not) are what MacIntyre calls the Characters of the Therapist, the Manager, and the Rich Aesthete. Space is not afforded to give a detailed treatment of each of these, but the basic point can be captured by thinking of these as caricatures of the types of leadership that garner followers (and which thus implies the type of leadership that will not). The Therapist is the figure who helps people come to terms emotionally or relationally with their life-situation, the Manager is the figure who effectively organizes people and tasks to measurable results, and the Rich Aesthete is the figure with means to please, to entertain, or to inspire. For extreme caricatures we might think of the motivational speaker, the CEO, and the media mogul. These labels coincide with careers that some of us may legitimately hold, and the existence of such persons and roles in society is nothing new; the point is not to critique these jobs in their own right, rather it is to make us aware that these have become the authorities that hold sway in our public and religious institutions, whether we have noticed them doing so or not.

So the result of the seismic shifts of modernity is not an authority vacuum but a flurry of new modes of influence that garner the authority. Most of the leadership resources of the past few decades can be categorized by one or more of these caricatures. That is not necessarily a bad thing, but it is also not morally or ecclesiologically neutral. If leadership has shifted from being a matter of accepting and wielding authority to gaining and exerting influence, we do just as well to note the temptations as the advantages. What happens to preaching or worship leading, for example, if the methodologies and purposes are borrowed from the entertainment industry? What happens to ministry teams and strategies if the means and ends are copied from the corporate worlds of profit and partisanship? What happens to pastoral care and discipleship if what we can do or say is measured by its preconceived therapeutic value? If we borrow unthinkingly from these modern modes of leadership we will inadvertently change the nature of the things we are leading, for better or for worse.

While it is not my goal in this studyguide to make an academic argument for or against modern modes of leadership, I do wish to promote critical and constructive engagement with the question of what is *good* about them. At the very least we need to be able to name unspoken premises, spot the cultural forces at work, and be wise to the social power dynamics at play, so that we can be faithful in leading the church of Christ in our time and place rather than a modern social group of our collectively self-interested choosing.

Returning to the question of this preliminary chapter, then, we can see that the question 'what is good about leadership?' has a complicated answer. It would be presumptuous to answer the question generally, as if leadership is good no matter what, as if one size fits all in terms of the match between leaderships and churches. To some degree we need to defer the question a bit longer, and simply conclude this chapter by noting that leadership can be made good by the grace of God. Leadership is good in that it is graciously provided for the ordering of persons and societies towards justice and peace in a fallen world, and church leadership is good as it attends to the particular means and ends of God which befit a Christian community. What that looks like in any given place and time will inevitably and properly be shaped to some degree by the language, culture, and leadership modes at hand, but not unthinkingly so. Even in Judeo-Christian cultures that appear to offer leadership models ready-made to copy and paste into church leadership, we must take care to follow Word and Spirit not only in discerning what is called for in any given circumstance, but what makes leadership Christian, and what makes church church.

Further reflection

On the spectrum below, locate (1) your experience of others' leadership, (2) your comfort level with being a leader, and (3) your theological view of church leadership:

| . . . . | . . . . | . . . . | . . . . |

    created good   provisional good less than ideal   necessary evil

What difference does servant leadership make to authority? Are they opposed?

What good might church leaders glean from the entertainment industry, corporate management, or the therapeutic arts? What might be unbefitting for a church?

Further reading

Thomas Aquinas, *Summa Theologiae 1a2ae*, 90–97 [1485].

Augustine, *City of God*, book XIX [426].

Paul Avis, *Authority, Leadership and Conflict in the Church*. London: Mowbray, 1992.

John Calvin, *Institutes of the Christian Religion*, book IV, [1560].

Marva Dawn and Eugene Petersen, *The Unnecessary Pastor: Rediscovering the Call*, ed. P. Santucci. Grand Rapids, MI: Eerdmans, 2000.

Stanley Hauerwas, *The Peaceable Kingdom: A Primer in Christian Ethics*. London: SCM, 1983.

Martin Luther, *On the Freedom of a Christian* [1520].

Alasdair MacIntyre, *After Virtue: A Study in Moral Theory*. London: Bloomsbury, 1981.

Martyn Percy, *Power and the Church: Ecclesiology in an Age of Transition*. London: Cassell, 1998.

Alec Ryrie, *Protestants: The Radicals Who Made the Modern World*. London: William Collins, 2017.

James W. Skillen, *The Good of Politics: A Biblical, Historical, and Contemporary Introduction*. Grand Rapids, MI: Baker Academic, 2014.

Sondra Wheeler, *The Minister as Moral Theologian: Ethical Dimensions of Pastoral Leadership*. Grand Rapids, MI: Baker Academic, 2017.

Jonathan R. Wilson, *Living Faithfully in a Fragmented World: Lessons for the Church from Alasdair MacIntyre's* After Virtue. Harrisburg, PA: Trinity Press International, 1997.

2

Confession: What Makes Leadership Christian?

It is clear that the good of leadership might be broadly defined but needs context in order to be filled out further. The good of leadership is inseparable from the concerns and circumstances, means and ends, of the group that is to be led. Even if different kinds of organizations might glean leadership tips from one another, a nation will not be governed the same way as a department store, a bank will not be run the same way as a band, and a church will not be led the same way as a choir. This may sound blatantly obvious, but it is surprising how often this flies under the radar when leadership resources are being appropriated for churches (let alone for faith-based non-profits). It might be nice if the point did not need belabouring, but it does. If you are already sold on this point you might skip to the next chapter, but it is probably worth sticking with me here, because the closer we look at the basic questions surrounding church leadership the more we find them fruitful for the guidance of our practice.

What makes leadership Christian, and what makes it churchly? Much ink has been spilt trying to take the measure of a Christian leader in the church, such that we might expect a really complicated answer to this question. At its core, however, the answer is actually quite simple. In his first letter to the Corinthians (which I take to be an inspired theological case study in church leadership), Paul the church planter has become aware of some local controversy about which leader to follow, and so he tackles this question head-on:

> It has been reported to me by Chloe's people that there are quarrels among you, my brothers and sisters. What I mean is that each of you says, 'I belong

to Paul', or 'I belong to Apollos', or 'I belong to Cephas', or 'I belong to Christ.'
Has Christ been divided? (1 Cor. 1.11–13).

Notice how Paul hooks the reader into the ranking system and then at the end
of the list inserts Christ. It is like he is saying: What will it be? Do you want your
rankings, or do you want *Christ*? You cannot have both. With the reconciling
Christ as the unifying head of the universal church, a beautiful diversity of
worship, discipleship, and leadership opens up before us in the contexts of time
and place. At the local church level the question is not whether you will belong
to this or that leadership model, but how our various callings fit together in
whatever body of Christ we serve.

If the temptation to pit leaders in competition with each other was intensified
for the church in the years of its founding, it is perhaps more complicated now
in the years of its fragmentation. In this studyguide we will not arbitrate between
various streams of Christianity but that should not be taken to suggest that such
differences are inconsequential. However, often we can get so attached to our
traditions and spiritualities that we are unable to recognize our fellowship with
others. Dividing lines between church traditions can run through local congregations as well. What used to be a matter of 'I follow Apollos' or 'I follow Paul'
can be reduced to something like 'I prefer hymns' and 'I prefer choruses', and so
on. While we should not trivialize these differences, we need to be careful not
to blow them out of proportion.

Certainly there are deep traditions and meanings behind such differences
that are not reducible to mere preferences or personality styles. However, we
have to continually ask ourselves how we might be illegitimately amplifying our
own inclinations and projecting them upon others as a grid for evaluating their
discipleship. Better yet, we ask Christ Jesus in the regular practice of confession,
both individually and corporately. This prompts us to empathy and helps us to
sharpen our understanding of what we and what others bring to the table.

If you are like me you will find some comfort in the notion that diversity
need not mean division, and that church leaders can be unified without having
to be uniform. When you rub shoulders with other church leaders, do you leave
feeling inspired to 'step up your game' or do you feel defeated, like you will never
measure up? It is one thing to aspire to the example of a mentor, but it is another
thing to fall for this competitive way of thinking that risks excluding the Christ
who reconciles.

Where does that leave us, however, when it comes to the discernment of true churches from false, or good leaders from bad? Does the blessing of something abstract like diversity leave the whole thing a bit open to chance or, worse, to deception? It may, but the warning of 1 Corinthians is that we had better not close ranks too quickly, or we are likely to close ranks on ourselves. Later in the letter Paul shows himself painfully aware of the dangers, but surprisingly minimalistic when drawing the baseline for detecting a Christian leader:

> You know that when you were pagans, you were enticed and led astray to idols that could not speak. Therefore I want you to understand that no one speaking by the Spirit of God ever says 'Let Jesus be cursed!' and no one can say 'Jesus is Lord' except by the Holy Spirit. (12.2–3)

That settles it then. A Christian leader is measured as one who says Jesus is Lord. But is that too simple? The apparent minimalism feels particularly problematic in our day, when Jesus' name is invoked to bless everything from a nation to a bakery, a political party to a military incursion. Even within the Christian faith, the church is so fragmented that there seems to be a church for every conviction, and a handful of cults on the fringe of every alternative. Surely the phrase 'Jesus is Lord' is more than an open password, the equivalent of clicking 'I am not a robot' before you enter a website and do whatever you want with it? To my mind this is not far from what we do when we separate the message of Christ from the means of church leadership, saying we must reach people with the gospel by whatever means necessary. It leaves a gap between theology and practice, between faith and works – and experience tells us that when God gives people an inch they tend to take a mile. I have to admit I am tempted to establish some other criteria in place of this simple confession – but then I might be in danger of denying Jesus' lordship myself.

In a real sense it is just as simple as that quote from 1 Corinthians 12 makes it sound. This pertains not only to our basic commission but also to our collaboration. There needs to be a genuine openness and generosity among Christians towards the manifold diversity of churches and approaches to leadership that take place within and across different cultures. If someone claims Jesus as Lord we need to take it seriously. If we have questions about their leadership we take it up in common confession as brothers and sisters, taking it seriously enough to submit our questions to them directly, seeking to bring our disagreements together before the Lord we both confess. This is the case no matter how doubtful things seem. In poker you might say this is 'calling someone's bluff', and sometimes it just might feel that way, but if we confess Jesus as Lord then it behoves us to humbly and genuinely take a person's word for it if they are confessing the same.

Within this shared confession we trust the same Lord to reveal to us our fellowship and to reconcile our differences over time. In the meantime we may be reconciled *to* our differences within that common trust in Christ, praying that we will be able to resolve our disagreements well. If other Christians have made decisions in their time and place that we cannot make in ours, but which we would be too hasty to comprehensively condemn on our own, perhaps the disagreement must be prolonged so that proper discernment and debate can carry on in good faith. In any case the confession of Jesus' lordship will be precisely what carries this along and unites us in hope and love. The most serious thing a Christian could say to another Christian would be not to recognize or respect their declaration that Jesus is Lord. As long as this declaration *is* respected, dialogue is open, and there is a measure of mutual blessing in the hope that in the Lordship of Christ we might yet see reconciliation in the particulars of doctrine or practice at stake. In that respect, it is just that simple.

But there is no either/or between the simple and the profound. The baseline statement *Jesus is Lord* is more than an open password; it is a public motto, a pivotal commitment, a gravitational centre, an ethical core. It is a claim to which churches and leaders hold themselves internally and ecumenically accountable, and which they also must try to make publicly intelligible without surrendering the integrity of its meaning. To say *Jesus is Lord* has implications in the extraordinary and the mundane. It is an all-encompassing statement. Jesus is Lord of everything or Jesus is Lord of nothing. We can come back to it every day and every moment and – like Brother Lawrence picking up a piece of straw as a 'practice of the presence of God' – we can see that it always applies.

For instance, if Jesus is Lord then daily bread is his to provide, which means the food on the table should never be taken for granted, but prayed for and received with gratitude. And if Jesus is Lord then this bread is received in relation to the needs of others, which one cannot presume the lords of national and economic distribution are always attending to Christianly. So the confession of Jesus' lordship even over the simplest of meals implies not only the grateful prayer for daily sustenance but also the submission of the entirety of one's economic relations to the reign of Christ. That is an example of how *Jesus is Lord* can be traced from personal confession to mundane action to socio-economic politics. The example can also be traced the other way around.

Simple does not necessarily mean unprofound, nor does it mean easy. The authors and recipients of the gospels and letters of the New Testament knew very well that the confession *Jesus is Lord* entailed a socio-political denial of the Empire's lordship which could make life uncomfortable, or even get a person killed. Not many generations have gone by since apostolic times where this has not been the case. In fact it is often when Christians sit most comfortably with their political situation that the claim of Jesus' lordship comes closest to crisis.

The twentieth-century examples of Nazi Germany and Apartheid South Africa still loom large in the social imagination as a signal of what might be at stake when the church loses sight of the comprehensively relativizing claim of Christ's lordship. In May 1934 when German evangelicals met in Barmen to form a response to Hitler's nationalization of the church, the Declaration they came out with went straight to the heart of the matter for Christians of all denominations, uniting them under one banner as the Confessing Church. It began by saying they were 'bound together by the confession of the one Lord,' and it went on to spell out in six theses what this meant. It was a rejection of the notion that 'there were areas of our life in which we would not belong to Jesus Christ, but to other lords' (thesis 2), and of the notion that the church 'could place the Word and work of the Lord in the service of any arbitrarily chosen desires, purposes, and plans' (thesis 6). In the hindsight of history we see that what might have seemed harmless at the time was a slowly mixed cocktail of religious presuppositions and incremental changes which eventually tipped over as a clear crisis of lordship. In many ways we have to admire the framers of the Barmen Declaration for seeing this crisis coming as early as they did, but even they would soon be saying it had been too little too late; too over-arching at the expense of specifics; too focused on the church's integrity and not focused enough on resistance for the sake of those about to become victims of the state. This was anticipated by the 1933 Bethel Confession, which Dietrich Bonhoeffer had helped draft but which he then refused to sign because it had been watered down beyond recognition. The irony of this is as thick as it is sobering, since the Bethel Confession itself rejected the notion that the cross of Christ could be 'regarded as a symbol for a generalized religious or human truth' (August version, section V).

The confession of Jesus' lordship can be as politically dangerous as it is deceptively simple. It is as comprehensively general and over-arching as it is relevantly particular to the mundane. It was reflection on such matters that led a group of South African church leaders to respond to the violence and politics of Apartheid with what was called the Kairos Document in 1985. It was not meant as the last word but as a clarion call to the ecumenical church to recognize that they faced a 'significant moment' (or *Kairos*) of truth in the lordship (or *Kyrios*) of Christ, and to prompt a united act of confession regarding the political situation at stake. We learn from these dramatic examples that the *Kairos* of Jesus' *Kyrios* is upon us all the time, and can often only be separated into the dramatic and the mundane as a matter of retrospect.

At any given moment we might be called by our circumstances to the confession of Jesus as Lord, even as a matter of life or death. But before it is called for by our circumstances we make it a regular habit of our personal and corporate lives. Not only do we confess Jesus as Lord daily in prayer and weekly in worship, but also whenever we revisit our doctrinal commitments, ethical positions, legal policies, leadership structures, ministerial arrangements, and vocational responsibilities. Every time we confess Jesus as Lord we deny the lordship of self and society, and confess to Christ our sins and our successes as well. This is the original and the perpetual mark of a Christian, and as such it is the mark of a Christian leader. In the run of daily affairs we might have any number of reasons to opt for the guidance of an Apollos over the guidance of a Peter or Paul – indeed the letter of 1 Corinthians goes on to suggest we might have to let divisions run their course so it can 'become clear who among you are genuine' (11.19) – but the mark of a genuine Christian leader is precisely that they maintain this confession.

When Jesus gave Peter 'the keys' that 'bind' and 'loose' earth and heaven and declared that 'on this rock I will build my church' (Matt. 16.18–19), it is often thought that he was handing over some kind of special authority or instrument for leadership. Some take it as the inauguration of an infallible church office, but moments later Peter is rebuked by Jesus in no uncertain terms (16.23). Others take it as a signal of the moral-hermeneutical task which would soon befall the apostles, but chapters later we see authorization to bind and loose being given to churches at large (18.15–20). So these views have some warrant, but the story itself points to something more basic. It is the first confession of Simon – 'You are the Messiah, the Son of the living God' (16.16) – that gets him the name Peter, the Rock on which Christ builds the church. It is in the context of two or three gathering for reconciliation in Jesus' name that we see people loosed from sin, and heaven bound to earth, in the practice of the presence of Christ (18.20). It is the first letter of Peter which calls the church 'a royal priesthood' built not on the author but on the 'living cornerstone', which is the Christ whose mercy they share (1 Pet. 2.4–10). The church leader is precisely the person who leads by confession of the lordship of Christ, not just in word but in practice. This brings with it a unique politic and practice which cannot be lost sight of no matter how good might be the leadership tips from other contexts and organizations and cultures.

By this I do not mean to suggest that in order for us to proceed with a book on church leadership we first need to establish a particular theory of organizational governance. Rather, the goal of this book is to set forth the vital impulses and basic parameters of church leadership which should be transferable and adaptable to any and every church. What goes for the fresh expression of church goes also for the historic traditions, even if different language and cultures and contexts will lead two different churches at any given time and place to look and feel very different from one another. There is in my view plenty of room for disagreement about how exactly to structure church governance, but threading through every expression there are constants that mark it as church. The discussion of these takes place under two very similar headings: the Marks of *the* Church and the marks of *a* church.

The historic Marks of the Church were established at the First Council of Constantinople in 381, when the Nicene Creed confessing 'one Lord Jesus Christ' had its third article extended to spell out the ramifications for the church: namely, that it be *one, holy, catholic, and apostolic*. This means that unity is tied up with sanctity, which is to say that the church is set apart and made righteous by the ever-renewing mercy of the Christ it confesses and serves. It also means apostolicity is tied up with catholicity (or universality); which is to say that the church is precisely not the expansion of a uniform empire, but the sending of missions to see Christ-confessing communities take root in all the diverse cultures of earth. Where two or three are gathered under Jesus' lordship the Church Universal is there; they are part of it and it is part of them. There is widespread agreement across all streams of the church today that ours is a union to be known in diversity, even while there are still some significant divisions yet to be reconciled when it comes to the way this plays out in faith and practice.

But what are the constants within this diversity? Is it enough to say church leaders will be united by their confession of Jesus as Lord, and then operate so diversely that there might be nothing recognizable about them? There is danger of understatement here, as it seems to suggest that churches could be more indecipherable from other religions than from one another. However, there is a danger of overstatement here as well. Retrospective analysis of the errors of empire and colonialism have rightly led to a chastening of our presumptions about what the constants of the international church really are. Too often and too easily there are cultural premises and practices that get so woven into the fabric of our churchly life together that we then insist on their duplication and refabrication even in places where those premises and practices are foreign and unnecessary. Missionaries need to know what makes a church, and then be careful not to over or understate the claim. This is true of church leaders who remain locally as well. So what are the orienting practices common to all churches? What are the essential practices that set churches apart as churches and thus give shape to the kind of leadership that they require? Along with the four historic Marks of the Universal Church, this is the question of the marks of a local church wherever it lands.

There is some variance as to the precise number and name of the marks of a church but they are typically covered under the headings of Word, Sacrament, and Discipline. Not only have these practices been typical, but there is biblical-theological precedent for saying it should be so. In the destabilized environment of the Reformation period it became rather important to reconsider and re-establish the marks of a church so that the ensuing diversification might still take place within defensibly *catholic* if not *Roman Catholic* bounds. So for instance Article 7 of the 1530 Augsburg Confession stated that while 'it is not necessary that human traditions or rites and ceremonies ... should be alike everywhere', the church definitively remains 'the assembly of saints in which the Gospel is taught purely and the sacraments are administered rightly'. Here we see the ministries of Word and Sacrament named explicitly, and by virtue of the descriptors 'purely' and 'rightly' we see the ministry of Church Discipline referred to implicitly. This threefold delineation was affirmed in the doctrine of John Calvin and the pastoral theology of Martin Bucer, and though there has been a variety of emphases and elaborations over time, these marks have remained in the backbone of the Body of Christ. To say so is not necessarily to be legalistic but to be *particular* about what it is to be the church in the world. To paraphrase Brother Lawrence and bring more specificity to the sociality of our existence, we might call these the essential practices of the presence of Christ. Where the Word is heard and discerned as the guide for life and salvation, where the sacraments (or ordinances) of baptism and communion are shared, and where the communion of believers submit themselves to the life of mutual discipleship – even before any of it is done perfectly – there is a church.

One of the quintessential scenes of the early church was in Emmaus, where two followers of Jesus came to grips with the new form of his presence in the aftermath of his death, between his resurrection and ascension. As the story goes in Luke 24, Jesus came to them on the road as a 'stranger', they told him of their dashed hopes that Jesus had been 'the one to redeem Israel', and 'beginning with Moses and all the prophets, he interpreted to them the things about himself in all the scriptures'. Still unbeknownst to them as Jesus, the stranger accepted their invitation to stay with them, and then it all came together:

> he took bread, blessed and broke it, and gave it to them. Then their eyes were opened, and they recognized him; and he vanished from their sight. They said to each other, 'Were not our hearts burning within us while he was talking to us on the road, while he was opening the scriptures?' ... Then they told what had happened on the road, and how he had been made known to them in the breaking of bread. (Luke 24.13–35)

This is the scene we were prepared for by Matthew 18.15–21, which promised Christ's presence wherever two or three would be gathered for the disciplined life of forgiveness and reconciliation, implying confession and repentance, in Jesus' name.

This is also the scene we should think about in John 20.29 when Thomas touched the wounds of the not-yet-ascended but definitely resurrected Christ, and Jesus said we would be blessed who are yet to come, who have *not* seen him in the flesh but have nonetheless believed. We may have a hard time thinking that our situation is somehow *blessed* compared to the first disciples – and we have good reason to long for the return of Christ in the flesh – but we should not miss the staggering nature of Jesus' claim, which is that we who gather to confess Jesus as Lord are practising the very presence of Christ. Even with the resurrected Christ physically walking and talking and eating with them, the disciples were learning that Jesus' presence would carry on in the sharing of Word and Sacrament and the submission of their lives to each other.

This is also the scene that the sign of Pentecost asks us to imagine springing up at tables and riversides in every language and nation under heaven since the birth of the church at the coming of the Spirit (Acts 2.1–13). When Paul said: 'no one can say "Jesus is Lord" except by the Holy Spirit', it depicted the diversity of churches in terms of neither a uniform institution nor an unintelligible connection. Confessing Jesus as Lord rather than ourselves, in faith we join with others under the sign of Pentecost and find that there are ways of saying Jesus is Lord we had not yet known by ourselves, even as we take joy that the marks of a church arise in diverse but recognizable forms among those once considered strangers, now revealed as friends. This is at the dynamic heart of the mission of God which envelopes and enlivens church leadership. We will take a closer look at that mission in the next chapter.

We confess Jesus as Lord. Not only does this stand at the beating heart of a leader's attitude and practice, but it also serves as a confessional reset that reorients us in the simplicity and the profundity of our calling. It offers a regular diagnostic that can set us up to tackle the complexities of various seasons and circumstances, both as individuals and as churches. The particular focus in this book is leadership in a church, that particular organization which is marked by the practice of perpetual Christ-confession. This is more than a secret password to be discarded as irrelevant upon entry. It shapes the very soul and social dynamic of the group. The one, holy, catholic, and apostolic Church throughout the world is going to be manifold in its beautiful diversity but unified in the faithful dynamics of attending to the Word, sharing the sacraments, and submitting one to another in the mutuality of discipleship. It is within these basic parameters that church leaders can begin to be more specific about the tasks at hand.

Further reflection

Does the confession 'Jesus is Lord' seem too easy or ill-defined to serve as a basis for recognizing other Christians and church leaders? See if you can imagine a local situation where it might fuel collaboration and encourage reconciliation.

On the other hand, do the practical implications spelled out in this chapter seem too rigid or over-prescriptive? See if you can imagine how something like Word or Sacrament might take creative shape in a totally different culture.

Would you add to or subtract from the traditional marks of a church? If there are any marks you would add, could you identify a traditional one to which they relate?

Further reading

'Barmen Declaration' in Eberhard Busch, *The Barmen Theses Then and Now*, trans. D. Guder and J. Guder. Grand Rapids, MI: Eerdmans, 2010.

'Bethel Confession' in Dietrich Bonhoeffer, *Dietrich Bonhoeffer Works 12: Berlin: 1932–1933*, trans. I. Best, D. Higgins, and D. W. Stott, ed. L. Rasmussen. Minneapolis, MN: Fortress, 2009.

Karl Barth, *The Church and the Churches*. Grand Rapids, MI: Eerdmans, 2005 [1936].

Eberhard Bethge, *Friendship and Resistance: Essays on Dietrich Bonhoeffer*. Grand Rapids, MI: Eerdmans, 1995.

Dietrich Bonhoeffer, *Dietrich Bonhoeffer Works 4: Discipleship*, trans. B. Green and R. Krauss, ed. G.B. Kelly and J.D. Godsey. Minneapolis, MN: Fortress, 2001 [1937].

Brother Lawrence, *The Practice of the Presence of God*, trans. R.J. Edmonson, ed. H.M. Helms. Brewster, MA: Paraclete Press, 1985 [1692].

Martin Bucer, *Concerning the True Care of Souls*, ed. P. Beale. Edinburgh: Banner of Truth, 2009 [1538].

John Calvin, *Institutes of the Christian Religion*, book IV, chapter I, [1560].

Christena Cleveland, *Disunity in Christ: Uncovering the Hidden Forces that Keep us Apart*. Downers Grove, IL: InterVarsity Press, 2013.

Edmund P. Clowney, *The Church*. Downers Grove, IL: InterVarsity Press, 1995.

Jon Coutts, *The Marks of a Church*, Cambridge: Grove, 2018.

J.C. Hoekendijk, *The Church Inside Out*, trans. I.C. Rottenberg, ed. L.A. Hoedemaker, and P. Tijmes. Philadelphia, PA: Westminster, 1966.

Willie J. Jennings, *Acts*. Louisville, KY: Westminster John Knox, 2017.

Lesslie Newbigin, *The Household of God: Lectures on the Nature of the Church*. London: SCM, 1953.

James B. Torrance, *Worship, Community and the Triune God of Grace*. Downers Grove, IL: InterVarsity Press, 1996.

3

Mandates: What Do Christian Leaders Do?

If church leadership is good, what is it good for? The marks of a church go some of the way to answering this question, but what are our mandates? What is our mission? At the end of 11 chapters of winding doctrinal discourse, the letter to the Romans wraps up with doxology, confessing that all things are from the Lord and through the Lord and to the Lord, forever. But that is not the end of it. Within the *from* and *through* and *to* of the Lord's merciful work there is a life to be lived and a church and a mission to join:

> I appeal to you therefore, brothers and sisters, by the mercies of God, to pre-sent your bodies as a living sacrifice, holy and acceptable to God, which is your spiritual [or reasonable] worship. Do not be conformed to this world, but be transformed by the renewing of your minds, so that you may discern [what is the good and acceptable and perfect] will of God. (Rom. 12.1–2)

Previous verses said none of us has 'known the mind of the Lord' – let alone 'been his counsellor' – but the fact of divine mercy is that God *has* come to be known by us as we share what we receive in the power of God (11.33–36). The grace of this knowing is not in each of us thinking *of* or *for* ourselves or by conforming to world patterns, but by ever-renewed discernment of God's will.

As we pursue the renewing of our minds in this regard it can be helpful to reflect on some of the ways that, despite our best intentions and culturally Christian backgrounds, we might already be conformed to this world. So in what follows we might find it helpful to contrast the central mandates of Christian life and mission with the basic ingredients of modern free-market liberalism outlined in Chapter 1. We do this not because the ways of the modern West are entirely incongruent with the ways of God, but because we believe we are always forming and reforming in the grace of Christ.

Few would disagree that the 'turn to the subject' that took place in the modern Enlightenment had some very good impulses and results to it that ought to be preserved and perpetuated. With this move has come an increased political respect for the dignity of the individual, which has engendered the contemporary focus on global human rights. For many centuries the 'subject' to which modernity turned was still the idealized productive white male, but in many pockets of the world the turn to the individual has eventually brought about a greater social justice for minority groups who have historically been repressed or exploited. This good work continues, and the church would be wise to discover where it has things to learn from society in this regard. Sometimes the Spirit sends pockets of our world out ahead of the church on a moral issue and allows that to be a rebuke to us. This is a possibility we should not shy away from due to a ham-fisted application of Romans 12's exhortation about nonconformity. There is no easy formula for negotiating our relationship to the world in this respect: we must be attentive to the ways and the works of God in the Word and in the world, seeking the renewing of our minds in fellowship with those brothers and sisters and others without whom God remains less than fully known.

Other times, however, a social movement takes place that is very much in accord with the Christian mission, but devolves into something that can then begin to be counterproductive. We see examples of such a thing in the conditions of late modernity, where whole societies are now so firmly organized around the guiding value of individual autonomy and the central premise of self-interest that it can have a perverse effect upon even those communities and projects which would not otherwise have made these things ends and means in themselves. We see this quite pronouncedly in churches that have slowly learned to orient the means and ends of worship, discipleship, and mission almost entirely around measures of effectiveness and numerical growth, which are themselves managed according to the assumptions of a consumerist age. If the prime mandate of Christian discipleship is that we look out for the interests of others, then how do we keep hold of that when the social contracts of our time so habitually run on the engine of self-interest? Must churches strap themselves to that engine to some degree in order to survive as a witness to society, or do they inevitably pollute their witness by doing so? Keep an eye out for this in what follows, contrasting it with the mandates for Christian life and mission that set the tone for biblical theology in the first books of both the Old and the New Testaments.

When it comes to the question of what leadership is good for, we must first situate ourselves within the basic instructions for navigating life on earth, which are found in the first few chapters of Genesis. We have already seen from Augustine and Thomas that there is rather a lot at stake in how we interpret the biblical story of creation. In an important sense this story extends right to the call of Abraham in chapter 12. These narratives are less concerned with modern-historical details and more concerned with framing human origins in terms of the God–world relationship. For our purposes there is one thing I wish to highlight briefly in these stories: namely, what the Creator deemed to be good, not good, and bad within creation.

The first bit is easy. What was good about creation? Genesis 1 says 'everything'. If the six-day layout of God's creative work shows us anything, it is the all-inclusive good of what God made. If it was not good, God did not create it. This is not to say that there was an eternal curiosity shop from which God chose pre-existent goods for the cosmic DIY project, but that God made and declared all good, all by God's self. When we zoom in on the creation story with Genesis 2, however, we see more nuance to this picture of goodness. First we see that the six-days are not everything, but the set up for what our life story is all about. Goodness is not complete on its own. The seventh day completes the picture by telling us what we are good for, which is to be hallowed; to be at rest with God; to be blessed (1–4). What we are good for is not greatness or autonomy but holiness; and the picture we get of holiness is not of a personally possessed perfection but of a dynamically sustained relationship with God and thus with the rest of creation. The best word for this is probably *shalom*; peace in its richest, fullest sense; a peace that can be perfect even as it grows in perfection, as finitude is caught up in the eternal goodness of God.

This picture is buttressed and filled in by what unfolds in the rest of chapter 2, where two things are marked off as *not good*: first, to eat from the tree of knowledge of good and evil, and second, for the human to be alone (17–18). Notice that it does not say God made anything that was not good, but that the goods God made could be put to use detrimentally. The individual human is still good, and even the notorious tree and its fruit is still good – the question is what is it good for? What is not good is for it to be utilized apart from its designated means and ends of *shalom*. The Creator may reserve the right to give more allowances and instructions as time goes on, but in the first instance the Creator's two pro-hibitions are very theologically telling: do not take the knowledge of good and evil upon yourselves, and do not go it alone.

Sadly, the remainder of the account is an explanation of how we got (and get) it wrong. The forbidden fruit is eaten by each person apart from the permission of God, precisely because the humans listen to nature and do what pleases them. They take upon themselves the determination and deployment of good, and so invite upon themselves and upon creation the experience of evil. Once evil is in the door, havoc is reeked. The humans are now unsafe in their individuality, experiencing the shame of the other's gaze in a world where none can be trusted to be good, let alone one's body. Human relations with nature and with each other are plunged into enmity and pain, collaborative dominion turns to com-petitive domination, and the spectre of death becomes something immanent, final, and thus frightening.

But by the grace of God, life goes on. From the provision of clothing and children to the expulsion from the tree of life (which limits evil's foothold) we get the clear impression that God intends to work within this tainted situation for the preservation of corrupted creatures, and even to their redemption (see 2.14—3.1). Thus it is that an Augustinian might consider leadership structures a provisional good for the redeemable management of creation's goods within the circumstances of enmity, or a Thomist might argue that leadership was always a good aspect of human sociality, but has taken new forms in the world because of sin and needs the influence of grace to pursue the good. Whether we side with Augustine or with Thomas, we can see from the creation narratives that the issue of leadership's goodness is measured on whether it attends faithfully to the command of God or insists on exacerbating and systematizing the not-goodness of having it our way.

We see the exacerbation of not-goodness in the infamous story of Cain and Abel as well, where one brother's offering is rejected, the other's is accepted, and things escalate quickly into murder. Moralistic retellings of this story tend to focus on the presumed lesser quality of Cain's offering or on the psychology of letting anger or jealousy fester, but as Genesis 4 tells it it seems that at that point, in God's view, things could still have gone either way. 'If you do not do well, sin is lurking at the door,' the Lord said to Cain; but 'if you do well, will you not be accepted?' (7). The initial rejection of Cain's offering was not necessarily the rejection of Cain for anything he had done wrong, but the flip side of God's election to bless them both through Abel. Cain could still 'do well' by God's blessing, but future offerings would presumably put the 'tiller of the ground' and the 'keeper of sheep' into an economic relationship to the glory of God (2–4). Had this been pursued, sin would have been 'mastered' and the brothers' work and worship could still have been well done (7). Instead, sin got its foot even further in the door.

A few generations later in Genesis 4 we see enmity not only flourishing but getting systematized. Cain had been made to wander the earth, and in the gracious judgment of God was protected by a mark that promised 'sevenfold vengeance' on any that killed the first killer and perpetuated his sin (15). But just like his ancestors before him Cain's great-great-great-grandson Lamech took matters into his own hands. In this case rather than the forbidden fruit or the sacrificial system it was the protective mark of vengeance that got put to humanity's own devices. Lamech promised to avenge whatever harm was done to him not seven but seventy-seven times over (17–24), and with this self-protective pre-emptive threat we have the makings of the prototypical empire: the systematization of original sin to privilege a patriarch with power. And, as Kurt Vonnegut so eloquently put it, *so it goes.*

By the time of Noah the rampant enmity was so thoroughly defying its God-given limits that it called for further divine limitation. God seems to flirt with the idea of just ending it all right there, but by way of a flood instead we get a shortened life-span and a creational 'reset', as it were, enacted by way of a special covenant with one of earth's peoples (Gen. 5—10). This covenant reiterated the original creation mandate to 'be fruitful and multiply, and fill the earth' (9.1), but a rainbow was put in the sky as a sign to remind God to stick with it, which turns out to be good news for us because the world would soon descend again into the self-making impulses of empire.

In Genesis 11 we see the people refusing to 'be scattered abroad', instead presuming upon heaven to build a tower and make a name for themselves. So we see at Babel that for their own good and ours they were hit with the confusion of languages, thus putting a limit on the extent of their self-perpetuating imposition of power and language upon the world (1–9). By God's grace and against our human inclinations, the filling of the earth went on, but apart from a centralized human power. For our own good we were divided and scattered, limiting our empire-building capacities and perpetuating the divinely ordained diversity of peoples across the earth – peoples who would with time be redeemed in the manifold goodness of God. We see this affirmed in the transition from Noah's covenant to Abram's, which forms the bridge from Genesis 1–11 to the rest of the Bible, wherein it is seen that through Abram's family 'all the families of the earth shall be blessed' (12.3).

Why do I relay this story of the original creation mandates and the covenants that were provided to deal with our sin? Because it is important to situate church leadership within the larger story of what leadership is good for, and what it is not. What is good is to serve the *shalom* of God in this world of enmity, which means carrying on with the cultural mandate to fill the earth and to steward it fruitfully – not to our own devices but in collaborative faithfulness to the command and provision of God. If we can put a name to the alternative temptation, the sinful impulse that is woven into the enmities of earth, we might call it this desire to take the good and make it great, to build empires and names for ourselves rather than delight in the humble service of God. That does not preclude celebrating when the ways and works of God flourish in numerical terms, but it does preclude measuring and managing things to that end. We are called not to be great but to serve the good that God has for us in God's own ways and time.

In the stories of creation and fall and throughout the Old Testament we learn from Israel that the road to *Sheol* is paved with best intentions. What seems good to us may not be in step with the living lead of God. Even in giving the ten commandments God begins with a command that puts the rest in their place: 'I am the Lord your God, who brought you out of the land of Egypt, out of the house of slavery; you shall have no other gods before me' (Ex. 20.2). These remain the command of the living God of Israel; they are not life-principles to be put to use as we see fit. God remains God, even of God's own command. If we turn them into blueprints to be copied or principles to be loosely improvised on our own, we tear them apart from the very fabric of *shalom* and of the ongoing grace of God.

Compare the creation mandate thus far with the presumptions of modernity and we are quickly confronted with the fact that the model of mutual service of God does not fit easily with the social contracts of mutually assured self-interest. We understand very well why self-interest exists and why, upon observation of the natural run of things, we should feel the need to come up with a society that manages it to something approximating the common good. But this does not excuse us from the need to reckon with patterns and presumptions of enmity and submit ourselves instead to the purposes of *shalom* inasmuch as they have been revealed and availed to us in Christ. This is not to say God cannot make the most of our modern systems of democracy and the mechanisms of the free market, but it is to say that we had better not confuse the means and ends of those things with the means and ends of the church.

Fast forward, then, to the first few books of the New Testament, where Jesus Christ is revealed as the fulfilment of the Law and the Prophets. This fulfilment does not nullify but enables the moral life of believers. It has not ceased to matter what we do. It is simply and gratefully the case that all we can do is accomplished for us and in us by the resurrected Christ. So it is that the Law and the Prophets have been appropriated in Christ to the good of creation and its fulfilment in new creation. This is the reality to which the church bears witness, and as long as time goes on, it is a work in which the church participates by the power of the Holy Spirit. The ramifications of this for church leadership are brought succinctly into focus by what have now become known as the Great Commandments and the Great Commission. In what remains of this chapter we will consider these briefly, and explore their relevance to the question of what leaders should do by bringing them to bear on the issue of time management.

According to Jesus the beating heart of God's purposes for creation could be summed up in a particular set of commands that God gave to the covenant people of Abraham. When asked to name the commandment to be considered above all, Jesus answered:

> The first is this, 'Hear, O Israel: the Lord our God, the Lord is one; you shall love the Lord your God with all your heart, and with all your soul, and with all your mind, and with all your strength.' The second is this, 'You shall love your neighbour as yourself.' There is no other commandment greater than these. (Mark 12.29–31)

This is part and parcel of Jesus' fulfilment of the Law and the Prophets: to fulfil all righteousness not only for us but in us, grafting all nations into the covenant people and liberating them for the love of God and neighbour in Jesus' name. Even before Jesus' death his disciples would have thought this a costly calling in a world spoiled by sin and embedded in enmity, but this was underlined for them when they reckoned with the cruciform path that Jesus walked. After Jesus' death and resurrection, however, it became clear that in some sense the best was yet to come.

At the end of Matthew (and echoed in the beginning of Acts) we see that the plan was for the resurrected Jesus to present himself in a new way, by sending the disciples to multiply and scatter their discipleship across the earth. Before his ascension:

> Jesus came and said to them, 'All authority in heaven and on earth has been given to me. Go therefore and make disciples of all nations, baptizing them in the name of the Father and of the Son and of the Holy Spirit, and teaching them to obey everything that I have commanded you. And remember, I am with you always, to the end of the age.' (Matt. 28.18-20)

There is plenty in this commissioning on which we could comment, but here we will simply take note of the basic tenor of what Jesus has in mind for his disciples: If the creation mandate was to scatter the earth with people serving God, and the covenant was for all the peoples of earth to be blessed through Abram's family, then the Christian fulfilment of this is to see that mission continue. Now that the Law was fulfilled in Christ, however, this would be a matter not of sacrifices and theocratic government, but a matter of mutual discipleship spreading from community to community, as diverse persons were baptized into communities defined not by their various empires of preference or politics but by discipleship together under the guidance of the living Lord Jesus Christ. In this there appears to be a place for teaching and baptizing and leading, but at every step the authority remains in Jesus' hands, and the shared pursuit of the disciples is that they would hear and obey Jesus' commands.

These commands do not come to us out of the blue but come to us with shape and form consistent with the rest of the ways and works of God. That does not mean they are blueprints handed over for us to build the kingdom or mass-produce churches according to some kind of apt growth model that seems to be working. Neither does it mean that our prior understanding of the ways and works of God is wholly correct or rightly applicable in every place and time. Yes, Jesus speaks to us today, and yes Jesus is the same yesterday, today, and forever, but the way Jesus speaks is not with a direct line to individuals who then relay his message in word-pictures and riddles. Nor is it with a static tradition or set of principles that we wield and apply as makes sense to us. Jesus speaks in the pattern of Revelation. 'These are the words [of Christ]', it says in one way or another in letters to seven different local churches (2.1,8,12,18; 3.1,7,14), and each time towards the end there is a common refrain: 'let anyone who has an ear listen to what the Spirit is saying to the churches' (2.7,11,17,29; 3.6,13,22). The pattern is instructive for us: God speaks to us in churches. What a humbling enterprise to take part in, let alone lead!

So it is that as Christian leaders we understand ourselves to be called to serve God faithfully within the societal structures and relations at hand, but not to sell our souls to them. Christians may participate in a free market democratic system which assumes self-interest, for instance, but that does not mean they should operate from a place of self-interest. We are called to live in these conditions in such a way that bears witness to the good of creation and to Christ's work of reconciliation, and one key way we bear witness to this is by gathering in diverse communions of grace to confess and obey Christ as Lord in real time together. The way of life this engenders has a particularly Christian shape to it, even if that shape is not prefabricated and plunked down into local communities in the same way every time.

The shape and the contours of Christian life and community are laid out for us quite neatly in the Great Commandments. The problem is in the details. It is one thing to love God with all my heart, soul, mind, and strength if all of those parts of my self are well-adjusted, and another thing entirely when they are disarranged and even feel like they are at war with each other. It is one thing to love my neighbour as myself when all the needs of my neighbours and family and friends are nicely compartmentalized in ways that do not conflict with each other, and another thing entirely when my prior commitments get interrupted by a man by the side of the road who needs my help.

These dilemmas appear to be anticipated in Luke's Gospel when, after hearing the Great Commandment, the lawyer asks Jesus who his neighbour is (10.29). We tend to give the lawyer a hard time for trying to 'justify himself' over this, but we can empathize with the dilemma he might have been feeling. Whether or not he was appealing to the problem of conflicting responsibilities, we can imagine the Priest and the Levite in Jesus' parable might have done so. The fact that Jesus holds out the example of the good Samaritan – the one who puts his other, presumably good, commitments on hold to help the wounded stranger – only accentuates the problem. It is a problem of time management that plagues church leaders constantly. There is no end to the neighbours to love; the question is not *whether* to love but *which*! Church leaders will have little problem filling their calendars with good things that could be done, even to the point of working sixty to seventy hours per week doing what seem like entirely good things for God – and most of it will look very good in an annual report. The question then is not so much *what* but *which* good thing to do. Before this is a time-management question, it is a theological one.

When this question comes up in conversation among church leaders you will often hear the rule of thumb, 'God first, family second, ministry third.' There are pastoral and practical reasons for this of course, foremost of them being the reason the question has been raised in the first place, which is usually because ministry responsibilities are eating too much into time with family or into devotional time with God. In that context the rule of thumb is meant as a rebalancing of priorities or a reminder to say no to some things. But how meaningful or sound is it as a rule of thumb? The Gospels of Matthew (10.32–42) and Luke (14.25–27) record times when Jesus seemed to suggest that his call to ministry was to come before family, and the Gospel of Mark (3.31–35) further blurs the lines. Sound biblical theology certainly suggests that, properly understood, service to God is not in competition with responsibilities to family or ministry, but that God is to be served in and through them.

Then there is the popular idea that so-called devotional time is always in competition with things such as study or work. What does it mean to love God with all my heart and soul if it is in competition with my body and mind? Does this leave me having to strike a balance on my own, or do four *alls* somehow add up to *one whole me* when given to God in love? Reflection on such matters might lead us back to the question whether we trust Jesus as fully as we might. Maybe we trust him to reconcile the cosmos to God, but can we trust him to reconcile our bodies to our souls, our hearts to our minds, our self-care to our callings, our various callings to one another? The Great Commandment seems to suggest not only that we can but that we must. We love God with all of that. We leave no stone unturned. We give it all to God and we pray to receive back from God what to do and the means to do it. We do not do this in isolation but with our neighbours and in prayerful consultation with Jesus – with Scriptures in hand and listening for the Spirit along with our local church. This is not a magical spell we can cast to achieve perfect balance in our lives, but it does provide a kind of rubric for praying about our lives and callings and discerning the things that God is asking us to do.

The story of Israel shows us a God who was way ahead of us on these problems. The Torah addressed everything from the Holy of Holies to the forgotten corners of daily life. The Ten Commandments addressed them in the concrete particulars of the various realms of worship, family, and neighbourhood. In speaking to ministerial students I have found it helpful to retrieve the basic rubrics of Lutheran theology for discernment of the various callings that God has placed in relation to one another in the ebbs and flows of our lives. In reflection on Scripture and tradition Martin Luther outlined three 'estates' within which Christians bore distinct responsibilities from God: political life (state government); economic life (home and work); and holy orders (church). More recently Dietrich Bonhoeffer broke them down further into four 'divine mandates' of government, work, family, and church, emphasizing that they are not fixedly established in natural law but diversely apportioned to us as callings of God. We will come back to these in Chapter 8, but they are worth mentioning now because of the reminder that church leadership finds its place and meaning within the larger cultural mandates of creation *and* the specific callings of God in our various lives. Church leaders do not discern their responsibilities in a vacuum but in relation to other God-given callings and responsibilities. Indeed, we might reckon it one of the primary tasks of church leaders to help their people to do the same. Church is, after all, where the Spirit calls people together to discern and to share in Christ's ongoing mission of reconciliation.

Thus the creation mandates and covenantal provisions of God work together with the basic commandments and commissions of the gospel as they are reconciled in Christ. This is not just a nice platitude; it actually has ramifications for how we organize ourselves not only as communities but even as individuals. If church is a participant in and a witness to Christ's reconciliation of the world to God, this entails not only the relay of a message but the very fabric of life, ministry and mission (2 Cor. 5.15–21). We look to Christ not only for the final reconciliation of all creation but also for the reconciliation of all the things in between. This is the faith we express when we give all of the self to God in love, and reckon that God asks us to serve by directing those efforts to our neighbours, our brothers and sisters, and even our enemies.

In the face of such all-encompassing divine mandates, what is a church leader to do? It is too easy for us to get the idea that we are supposed to take the Great Commandment and the Great Commission and to run with them, forgetting that they are done by us together, not any one person alone. But we have to remember the basic impulses of creation and covenant, and the way they are fulfilled and extended to this day in Christ. It is not our place to build an empire of self-interest or to sort out a self-help strategy for living and leading. That would take us right back to the original sins. Church leadership is not simply a matter of using whatever means necessary to convey a message that is ultimately detachable from the mode of delivery. Church leadership goes astray when it divorces itself from the whole thrust of what it is good for: from attention to *how* things 'work together for good for those who love God' (Rom. 8.28). Our place is not to go it alone but to gather in Jesus' name to love God, love neighbour, and scatter as many local bodies of Christian discipleship as the world can handle, baptizing and teaching and discipling one another as a witness of reconciliation.

Christian leadership means accepting a particular calling *as one of the group*, exercising the gifts of the Holy Spirit that are given for the purpose of following Jesus together, as we are formed into a community of self-giving, other-receiving love that bears witness to the grace of God in a systemically selfish world. If church leadership is good, that is what it is good for. If it all seems a bit overwhelming, that might not be a bad thing. If what we do is anything, it is a work of God in which we participate by grace.

Further reflection

Does leadership feel to you like an isolating or an onerous responsibility? What does it mean to you to reflect on what God in creation forbade and called not good?

Are you convinced that we must pay close attention to the prior commands of God but not turn them into principles that we wield for ourselves? What are the dangers here? Are there any dangers in letting go of any abiding principles whatsoever? Is a dependence on personal intuition or conscience any less potentially idolatrous than a reliance on religious habits or rules?

Do you feel like your heart, soul, mind, and body are at odds with each other? If you had to rank them in terms of the focus they get in your life, or the health of their relation to God, how would that look? Pray about what it means to love God wholly.

Does it help to think of politics, economics, family, and church in terms of callings to be received from God? Do you feel like these are in conflict? How would you rank them in terms of their clarity of focus in your life? Pray about this.

Further reading

Benedict, *The Rule of St. Benedict*, trans. J. McCann. London: Sheed and Ward, 1976 [530].

Dietrich Bonhoeffer, *Dietrich Bonhoeffer Works 3: Creation and Fall*, trans. D.S. Bax, ed. J.W. Gruchy. Minneapolis, MN: Fortress, 1997 [1937].

Dietrich Bonhoeffer, *Dietrich Bonhoeffer Works 6: Ethics*, trans. R. Krauss, C.C. West C.C. and D.W. Stott, ed. C.J. Green. Minneapolis, MN: Fortress, 2005 [1949].

Emil Brunner, *The Divine Imperative: A Study in Christian Ethics*, trans. Olive Wyon. London: Lutterworth, 1937.

Stanley Hauerwas and William H.Willimon, *Resident Aliens*. Nashville, TN: Abingdon, 1989.

Jonathan Leeman, *Political Church: The Local Assembly as Embassy of Christ's Rule*. London: Apollos, 2016.

Robin W. Lovin, *Christian Realism and the New Realities*. Cambridge: Cambridge University Press, 2008.

Martin Luther, *Book of Concord: The Large Catechism*. St Louis, KY: Concordia, 1952 [1529].

Roy McCloughry and Wayne Morris, *Making a World of Difference: Christian Reflections on Disability*. London: SPCK, 2002.

Kathryn Tanner, *Christ the Key*. Cambridge: Cambridge University Press, 2010.

Part 2

Means

4

Imitation: Does the Bible Show Us How to Lead?

As we turn to the vital practices of church leadership, let me begin with *The Simpsons*. There was a scene in episode seven of season five of this cartoon series that my brothers and I have never forgotten, because we have referenced it jokingly ever since we first saw it as teenagers in 1993. In it the Simpson family and what appears to be the entire town of Springfield are assembled to hear a motivational speaker named Brad Goodman, who ends up bringing young Bart Simpson onto the stage and upholding him as an inspirational example to them all. The joke is on the self-help guru, of course, since as a visitor to the town he has little idea how opposite to a role model Bart Simpson really is. But it is a credit to the speaker's rhetorical and motivational skills that he is able to take every cheeky comment Bart makes and turn it into a platitude for success. The satirical scene is written brilliantly by George Meyer, because it has the self-help guru begin by addressing the pressure to people-please, carry on by praising the self-expression of young Bart, and then finish by making a thickly ironic appeal to the crowd that they should all try to be more like the boy. When he entreats them to 'be like the boy' the crowd begin to chant 'Be like boy! Be like boy!' – first altogether and then 'just the ladies'(!) – until it ends with all eyes on 'the seniors in the back', who are heard for the first time chanting 'We like Roy! We like Roy!' My brothers and I used to like to chant this light-heartedly at the dinner table when Mom or Dad gave one of us some unsolicited praise. But after my baptism and subsequent path into pastoral ministry a few years later, the scene also continued to enter my mind whenever I encountered exhortations to church leadership that suggested I do it just like somebody else. Even as I felt this immense inner pressure to live up to the model of success held before me – *Be like boy! Be like boy!* – I would thankfully hear another inner voice whimsically whispering *We like Roy! We like Roy!* With that I would be reminded to think twice before I turned helpful examples into heroes or models or measures of success.

Unfortunately, this humorous dose of perspective was not always enough to rescue me from the crushing weight of impostor syndrome and self-defeat that I would feel as unrealistic models of success were held up for me everywhere I turned. Even when one knows in one's mind that the models are overly idealistic, in vulnerable moments one's heart can still be the last to know. Even when testimonies are couched in humble stories of the long dark night of the soul when nothing in the church seemed to be working out right at all, when the conclusion nine times out of ten is how it finally worked out and the church is numerically growing, then one still gets the idea that this is how pastoral work is ultimately measured. I do not mean to be cynical, it is just that I have attended enough of these sessions over the decades to know that for every good idea or re-energized leader these inspirational stories create, there is another person who leaves the room carrying the wounds of some collateral damage. This is not necessarily the fault of the speaker or the organizer, since it tends to relate more to the church-wounding premises of our marketing culture than to the particulars of the event itself – but the framing of these stories can do damage nonetheless.

There are two kinds of damage done by leadership models that are organized implicitly or explicitly around the aspiration of effectiveness: the damage of not measuring up, and the damage of success. In the first case, those deemed unsuccessful are doomed to a life of regular relocation, doubtful glances, patronizing advice, or worse, the spiritualization of self-loathing despair. In the second case, those deemed successful face the very real temptation to rely on themselves, not to mention the temptations that inevitably come with power, including decreased accountability. In both cases there is the danger of curving in on the self, either introspectively or programmatically. We need to grow in grateful dependence on God, and gracious interdependence with others, no matter how we measure up.

But what about learning from examples? Does the Bible recommend we look at contemporary practices or biblical narratives and take from them models for leadership? The New Testament is certainly unafraid to recommend imitation, even when it puts us up against an impossibly high standard. In Ephesians 5.1 it says to 'be imitators of God'. In 1 Corinthians, after diluting their urge to over-identify with him or Apollos or Peter (3.1–23), Paul still appeals to the church people to 'be imitators of me' – for which purpose he has apprenticed and sent them Timothy (4.16–17). In 1 Thessalonians the church of Thessalonica is commended for having become 'imitators' of the apostles, of the Lord, and of the churches in Judea (1.6; 2.14). We thus see the precedent for writings such as *The Imitation of Christ* by Thomas à Kempis, which begins with the exhortation to 'study to make [one's] whole life conformable to that of Christ' (I.1.2). The most famous line of the book says 'humble knowledge of one's self is a surer way to God than a deep search after knowledge' (I.3.4), and the complementary point that comes soon after says to 'seek rather to be instructed by one that is better, than to follow thine own inventions' (I.4.2). There is clearly a place for Christian role models and advisors – and there is no sense in flinching from it just because of the psychological damage of having been unhealthily measured against the successes of another.

With this theological perspective in place, in this chapter we explore a few of the leadership examples of the Old Testament and ask ourselves whether we are convinced they are meant to be followed and, if so, what can be gleaned from them. With each we will look for an affirmative echo from the New Testament and point out one or two threads of practical wisdom that could be considered exemplary for church leaders today.

Moses learns from Jethro to spread out the work – Exodus 18.13–27

By the time we come to chapter 18 in the Exodus narrative it has become clear that Moses has been chosen to lead the Hebrews out of Egypt, through the wilderness, and to the Promised Land. Moses' calling was a slightly unusual one, since it really got going when he murdered a slave-driver and went into exile in Midian, and there was confronted by the voice of God coming from some flaming shrubbery. That it has become known as a 'burning bush' is slightly unfortunate, since the remarkable things is that 'the bush was blazing, yet it was not consumed' (Ex. 3.2). The point is that the 'unburning bush' does not appear to need fuel for its fire, which foreshadows the fact that Moses will not require eloquence to speak for God (4.10–13). When Moses lacks the faith to accept this, God is angry but undeterred, and offers a compromise. Moses will still speak the words of God, but in public will be given the help of a fluent orator: his brother Aaron (4.14–17). So it goes that Moses returned to Egypt from Midian, led the people out, and started to get the point. 'The Lord is my strength and my might' was the song that accompanied Moses' first steps of freedom and carried his leadership into the wilderness (15.2). Soon God had Moses making bitter water sweet by throwing a chunk of wood into it (15.25), making water come from a rock by hitting it (17.6), and helping his men fight off invaders by keeping his hands held up in the air (17.11). Apparently it was enough to give Moses the impression that he could do anything and everything by himself – which brings us to the leadership lesson of Jethro.

In chapter 18 we see Moses reunited with his wife Zipporah and their two sons, who had been left in the safe-keeping of Jethro, her father the priest of Midian. Upon hearing of their delivery from slavery, Jethro confesses Moses' Lord as 'greater than all the gods' and they have the kind of blessed fellowship that the nations were meant to have with Abraham's people (1–12). The next day Jethro puts on his father-in-law hat and gives some advice. After watching Moses sit alone from dawn to dusk settling the people's disputes and giving them God's instructions, with a queue of people standing there awaiting a hearing, Jethro cannot contain himself. He says:

> What you are doing is not good. You will surely wear yourself out, both you and these people with you. For the task is too heavy for you; you cannot do it alone. Now listen to me. I will give you counsel, and God be with you! (18.17–19)

Affirming Moses' role as mediator and teacher (19–20), Jethro then adds his recommendations:

> Set such men over them as officers over thousands, hundreds, fifties, and tens. Let them sit as judges for the people at all times; let them bring every important case to you, but decide every minor case for themselves. So it will be easier for you, and they will bear the burden with you. (18.21–22)

In the events that follow we do not get a divine pronouncement for or against this advice, but we do see God work with it. This is not framed as a concession (as was the provision of Aaron), nor is it elevated to the level of universal principle. It is practical wisdom that is fit to be taken up in the fear of the Lord and deployable towards *shalom*. As a matter of fact that seems to be precisely what Jethro himself has in mind. His final appeal is that 'if you do this, and God so commands you, then you will be able to endure, and all these people will go to their home in peace' (23).

There are threads of leadership wisdom here, and we begin our running list by identifying two.

1 *Moses accepts counsel from an experienced person from outside his faith community.* This might come as a surprise given how many times such a thing is frowned upon in the Old Testament, but here we see outside counsel neither rejected outright nor set up as a universal good. A few factors may have contributed to this: although Jethro was a foreign priest he nonetheless respected Moses' Lord, was hospitable to Israel, and gave instructions that were answerable to God's command (23).
2 *Moses identifies and authorizes people to whom he will delegate tasks and decisions without abdicating his overall responsibility.* They will 'bear the burden with' him by bringing him 'every important case' and deciding 'every minor case themselves' (22). Moses seeks them out from among the faith community and empowers them because they are capable, they 'fear God, are trustworthy, and hate dishonest gain' (20–21). In other words, they submit their practical wisdom to the wisdom that begins and ends with the fear of the Lord.

The New Testament underlines these threads of wisdom with similar examples of its own. On the first point we have Paul in Athens, who discusses the things of God in the language of the people wherever he goes – be it the 'devout persons' in the Jewish synagogue, the people who frequent the 'market-place', or the 'Epicurean and Stoic philosophers' who assemble on Mars Hill (Acts 17.16–18). Whether or not this gives licence to borrow leadership practices and priorities from each of those places is a matter for further discernment, there is no doubt that Paul's example encourages us to 'look carefully' into the practices and beliefs of others and bring them into conversation with our understanding of the revelation of God in Christ (17.22–31). In this Paul risked ridicule from both sides, seeming to accept pagan worship as unwitting praise of God (23), and sounding to the philosophers like a 'babbler' (18–19). In 1 Corinthians Paul explains: 'I have become all things to all people, so that I might by any means save some. I do it all for the sake of the gospel, so that I may share in its blessings' (9.22–23). Those that assume 'any means' implies 'anything goes' should look closely at Paul's refusals elsewhere to let the ways of synagogue, market-place, or philosophy dictate the ways of the church (see Gal. 2; Acts 19.23–41; 1 Cor. 11.17–34; 1 Cor. 1—4). At the same time, Paul's interpretation of his own example shows that shutting out other languages and cultures may keep both us and them from a share in the gospel's blessings.

On the second point, related to work-sharing and delegation, not only does the New Testament affirm such wisdom but also significantly particularizes it to the unique tasks and spiritual dynamics of the church. We will have occasion to revisit this in later chapters, but the classic text to point to in this regard is Acts 6, when the twelve disciples chose seven more to help them in the dispersal of ministries that were arising in the early church. When we look closely at the story we see that the twelve had a secure understanding of their primary responsibilities, but did not use that to excuse a lack of responsiveness to increasing numbers and the material needs of the burgeoning Christian community (6.1–2). In a period of rapid change some people had begun to fall through the cracks, and those who noticed framed it as a matter of discrimination: minority Hellenists thought their widows were being neglected by the majority Hebrews (1). We do not have a record of whether this complaint was acrimonious or disputed at length, but from the rapidity of the transition to action we get no sense of defensiveness. The disciples' agreement is assumed, but it creates a dilemma of early church management. 'It is not right', the disciples tell the community, 'that we should neglect the word of God in order to wait at tables' (2). They select seven men who will be appointed the task, so that the part of attending to the material needs of the socially excluded will be taken care of without jeopardizing the part devoted 'to prayer and to serving the word' (3–4). This is an important check on a number of misleading impulses still faced in church leadership today: Moses' impulse to just add to his own workload, and the disciples' temptation to divert from their primary commission to take on what could be shared.

The example of Acts 6 combines our lessons from Exodus 18 in a poignant way. The whole episode is a response to growth in numbers, and the impression the text gives is that the church will attend to growth dynamics without sacrificing the church's integrity in the process. Like Moses, the twelve look for helpers who are fit for purpose, but in this case they ask the community to select them, and give direction regarding the kind of people they need. There is nothing derogatory about 'waiting on tables'; the positions require not just 'good standing' but fullness 'of the Spirit and of wisdom' (6.3). Those selected are then prayed for and commissioned with the laying on of hands, which shows an investment of trust which will be respected by both the receivers and the givers of the call to ministry (6). In the selection process itself we see the conviction that if the numbers of disciples are to increase in Jerusalem, it will be in tandem with the continuing spread of the word of God (7), and will not be to the detriment of the minorities and socioeconomically-excluded people who so easily fall through the cracks in the name of growth.

Sadly, it is one of the seven, Stephen, who becomes the first of the church's martyrs. Those serving widows are on the front lines, poking the gospel where it does not belong, messing with the social balance of religion and of Empire (8). The stakes and the demands are high; so should be the preparedness of the servants, in both competence for humble service required, and in wisdom of Word and Spirit (see Acts 7). The fate of Stephen might have been meant to dissuade the growth of the early church, but the disciples 'went from place to place, proclaiming the word' (Acts 8.4), spreading into other cultures (25–40). If there was any impulse to bunker down like Babel, centralizing around a mega church and their celebrity apostles, the Spirit of the early church was going to have none of it.

Deborah shares the lead with Barak – Judges 4.1–14

You may have noticed that Moses and the disciples looked for men rather than women to share the burden of leadership with him. This was standard in ancient times, and could just as well have been a concession to cultural norms as a principle God meant to lay down for all time. In any case, in the book of Judges we run up against one of the Bible's exceptions to the norm. There will have been any number of socio-economic reasons for male headship in ancient times, but when the Bible gives an exception we must take notice and revisit the so-called 'rule'. One such case is Deborah, who is presented to us in Judges 4 not only as a 'prophetess' like Moses' sister Miriam (Ex. 15.20) but also 'judging' like Moses' men had done (Judg. 4.4). As with Jethro's instructions before, there is nothing explicitly recorded to say that Deborah's judgement was either demanded or rebuffed by God, but the implication is that it brought a welcome reprieve from the years of evil sandwiching it on either side (4.1–3; 5.31–6.1).

What happens is that Deborah summons Barak and relays a command from God to draw up an army against the oppressor, but Barak refuses to go without her (4.6–8). Deborah agrees to go, but says that because of this Barak will not get the glory; instead it will go to a woman (9). What seems at first like a veiled reference to the glory that Deborah will take in his place ends up being fulfilled in Jael, the woman who finishes the army commander off with a tent peg (15–23). As it turns out, Deborah is the kind of prophetess and judge who is willing not only to share leadership with the reluctant Barak, but then to sing the victory song as a duet instead of a solo (5.1), which would have been well within her rights. Given the prominence and the pattern of this story in the days before Israel's kings, there is good reason to add Deborah to our models for leadership as follows:

3 *Deborah led without need for glory, served faithfully in partnership, and was not deterred from God's call by any adversity with social norms.* What we see in Deborah's story and song is that a woman was given a voice for God and used it to sing a duet to the glory of God (5.2–23), laying the blessing at the feet of an unlikely commoner (24–31). By this point in the book of Judges, any reader who is paying attention will have noticed a kind of a pattern. God has developed a habit of delivering the people through the unlikeliest of unlikely leaders, whether it is Othniel the younger brother to the star (Caleb, 3.9–11), Ehud the filthy left-hander (3.15–30), or Deborah who sits off the spotlight (4.4–5). It turns out not to be a habit God gives up easily.

New Testament examples that run along similar lines may include women like Phoebe or Junia (Rom. 16.1–2, 7), the latter of whom was considered 'prominent among the apostles' but who was only mentioned once. They would have been like the first disciples, whom Jesus called out of quotidian jobs and simple places, immersed in a travelling apprenticeship, and authorized to teach and lead upon his departure (Matt. 4.12–25; 10.1–42). On one occasion Jesus gathered not just the famous twelve but an unnamed seventy, sending them out in pairs to proclaim his kingdom (Luke 10.1–11). Jesus did not call these disciples out of their mundane lives to thereafter live alone above the fray. Whenever we see them they are not sages on hilltops, isolated and aloof, but continue to fish and be hosted in homes, even as they are steeping themselves in Scriptures and being sent on missions. In them we can see the thread of wisdom gleaned from Deborah, fulfilled and affirmed in the lordship of Christ. We also see this in the way leadership of the Ephesian church is passed on to the next generation – to Timothy through Eunice and Lois and Paul – but we will come back to this once we have considered the example of David on his way to becoming king.

David waits on Saul – 1 Samuel 24.1–13

We have already observed God's disappointment with Israel's request for a king, which both Samuel and the Lord took as a rejection of God's chosen manner of sovereign leadership through prophets and judges and priests (see 1 Sam. 8). However, we know that not only did God go ahead and give them a king (with some warnings and caveats of course), but invested the appointment with significance. Ultimately, we know that God would retain kingship for himself, but now he would rule through the ups and downs of Israel's kings, typified in the Davidic line which would be fulfilled in the God-man Jesus Christ. But we are getting way ahead of ourselves. At the point when God first enacts this process it takes the form of giving the people what they want, and having them come to grips with the fact that they may not really know what they are thinking (1 Sam. 9–10). As it turns out, their first king Saul does enough to be rejected by God (15) and replaced in the anointing of David (16), when Samuel is told not to look at 'outward appearances' but to look at the heart with the Lord (16.7).

What is particularly awkward and instructive for us about the anointing of David is that it takes place while Saul is still king, and comes with no set date for the transition, thus plunging David into the situation of waiting. David may not have been the most perfect of role models once he became king, but it is in this period of patient anticipation that he manifested the 'heart' God was looking for in an exemplary manner. We see this throughout David's persistent service to King Saul, but the scene which encapsulates it all is the potential showdown found in 1 Samuel 24. There we have David's example for aspiring leaders writ large:

4   *David accepted the call to leadership as it came to him from God, refusing the rush of ambition and resisting the temptation to seize power before it was properly given.* This was not easy. David could easily have justified the seizure of Saul's kingship by appealing to the misconduct of Saul, to the legitimacy of his own anointing, to the will of the people, or to the intent to do right by the kingdom. But at the height of such temptation David refused to do wrong to make a right.

The scene is almost as comic as it is tragic. In 1 Samuel 24 we see Saul pursuing David into the desert with an army of 3,000 men, and the tension is thick when the narrator tells us how close Saul gets without even knowing it. We can imagine ourselves with David deep in a cave as one of his companions whispers to him that Saul is right outside taking a toilet break (24.3). We can imagine how true it might sound when the man interprets this as the day when this king-turned-enemy is finally handed over by God to his successor (4). We can imagine all this and probably think of opportune moments in the social dynamics of a group or a church where it would be similarly possible and even in some way justifiable to pull off a coup, to swing the room in our favour, to undermine the leader, or to take charge before our time. But we might also recall that a leadership role is something we submit to as given, not usurped. If it is a *takeover* it is on the wrong foot from the get-go, diseased by the corruption of power. Even if circumstances are not quite so dramatic, for God it goes to leadership's heart.

As the story goes, 'David went and stealthily cut off a corner of Saul's cloak', only to be 'stricken to the heart' before the Lord, confessing to his men that it would be unbecoming to the God he served to lift his hand against his king (4–6). David could easily have turned a blind eye and let others do his dirty work for him, but back inside the cave he rebukes any such impulses and orders the men not to attack (7). Instead he steps out of the cave and calls out his loyalty to the king, his refusal of vengeance, and his hope to be vindicated and upheld by God alone (8–15). This ends the conflict (for the time being) and leads to the repentance and blessing of Saul (16–21). David accepts this but the fact that they go their separate ways shows a level of wise caution and respectful distance on the part of the one waiting in the wings (22). If there's a bit of solid advice here it might be that if it is not your time to lead, serve well; but if God has called you to it then let nothing stop you from due process – neither the temptation to shortcuts, nor the threats of naysayers.

A prime New Testament illustration of this is found in the letters of Paul to Timothy. In many ways closer to our contemporary situation than the examples of ancient Israel, the letters show an established church in Ephesus grappling with the passing on of the torch of leadership. Paul is the apostle who planted the church, and Timothy is his 'loyal child in the faith' who has been instructed to stay there to teach with 'love that comes from a pure heart, a good conscience, and sincere faith' (1 Tim. 1.1–5). This is contrasted with those posers to the pastorate whose ambitions turn them to 'meaningless talk' that wins people over more for its assertiveness than its depth of understanding (1.6–7).

Putting the two letters to Timothy together we get the picture that these competitors for Ephesian church leadership appear to have been getting into homes and deceiving uneducated women into the presumption of authority and a 'counterfeit faith', just as Paul was experiencing elsewhere (1.18–2.15; 2 Tim. 2.14–3.8). If so it would seem that something about early Christianity was making it possible for some men to persuade women to take a lead in their churches, whether – as in Timothy's case – those churches already had teachers or not. So when Paul infamously informs Timothy that he does not permit women 'to teach or have authority over men' but instructs him to 'let a woman learn in silence with full submission' (1 Tim. 2.11–12), we might assume it is a timeless principle reinforcing the universality of male-only leadership, but he is explicitly affirming the education of women and open to their leadership as elsewhere. What we should hear in the call to submission is a word for all students – especially those who have been systematically ignored for too long: learn!

In context, what Paul is not permitting these women is their *usurping* of authority (2.11), such that the reference to Adam and Eve is not a reference to the masculinity of leadership but the illustration of what happens when the second does not learn well from the first (13–14). For the women in Paul and Timothy's churches to carry on with their motherly roles as well as their education, but 'continuing in faith and love and holiness, with modesty' (15) is thus not only a specific exhortation for that time and place but a model for aspiring leaders. One who would become a leader needs to prepare in a way consistent with what that leadership will revolve around and entail. In this case that means learning the Word from the people entrusted to pass it on to you, and practising faithfulness in all of life. Leaders have first to be good followers. In 2 Timothy Paul draws on illustrations from military training to athletics to farming in order to say that you do not become a soldier without looking to impress an enlisting officer with behaviours distinct from civilian affairs, you do not win a competition without learning the rules of the game, and you do not take first share of the crops if you have not put in the work (2.1–6). How much formation and education one might need will be relative to the leadership responsibilities being accepted, but there should be no escaping the pastoral exhortation to submit fully and humbly to theological learning and spiritual formation before presuming to lead a church. It is also incumbent upon churches to protect those leaders they have commissioned, and to nurture a new generation.

I began the chapter by casting some doubt on the contemporary use of 'models' for leadership, but clearly the Bible indicates that it is vital for us to have other leaders nurture us in the faith, entrust us with leadership, and leave us with good examples to follow. However, we must also be mindful of what happens when we elevate leadership out of reach, crushing potential leaders under the weight of unrealistic expectations or offering them all hoops and no ladders. Paul joined Eunice and Lois in training Timothy and told him to 'let no one despise [his] youth' (1 Tim. 4.6–12). If anything, this reflection on the import-ance of leadership models should serve as a clarion call for careful teaching and caring mentors, rather than a recommendation of leadership blueprints. Moses and Barak may have lacked the faith to step up and do what God instructed, but instead of insisting they be heroes God graciously gave the advice of Jethro and the solidarity of Deborah, the voice of Aaron and the timely tent peg of Jael. Jethro and Deborah and Paul were not gods to Moses and Barak and Timothy, but that doesn't mean they were not God-sends.

All of this goes to show the importance of *both* models *and* discernment. Consider that earlier quote from Thomas à Kempis's *Imitation of Christ* in full:

> It is much better to avoid being precipitate in our actions, or clinging strongly to our own opinions. We should not believe all that we hear, nor gossip about what we hear of others. Listen to wise and sensible advice and be guided by someone better than you, rather than following your own opinions. Experi-enced people understand what they are talking about. The more humble and pleasing we are to God, the more we are at peace in all that we are doing. (I.4.1–2)

To reflect further on this, next we will continue in a similar vein by considering some *bad examples* of biblical leadership, so that we can get a handle on the basic posture (Chapter 5) and essential habits (Chapter 6) of a church leader in the conclusion of the first half of this book.

Further reflection

Can you identify a leader you admire, a role model you look up to, or a mentor or teacher who has helped you find your way? Give thanks for them, and for one or two things you have learned from them that are worth remembering.

Can you identify any burdens of expectation that might be weighing you down, or measures of success that might be leading you off track? Confess them to the Lord, and ask the Spirit to sift wise examples from faulty measurements.

Do you tend to rely more on your intuition or on attention to the practices of others? How might the former be more culturally influenced, and the latter more personally selective, than it first seems?

Reflecting on the examples of leadership that have been gleaned from this chapter, take note of one or two that seem particularly applicable to your current situation, and see if you can write a prayer or share with a colleague what you have learned.

Further reading

Thomas à Kempis, *The Imitation of Christ*, trans. Robert Jeffery. London: Penguin, 2013 [1427].

Walter Brueggemann, *The Creative Word: Canon as a Model for Biblical Education*. Philadelphia, PA: Fortress, 1982.

Ellen F. Davis, and Richard B. Hays, eds, *The Art of Reading Scripture*. Grand Rapids, MI: Eerdmans, 2003.

Liz Goddard and Clare Hendry, *The Gender Agenda*. Downers Grove, IL: Inter-Varsity Press, 2010.

Eugene H. Peterson, *Five Smooth Stones for Pastoral Work*. Grand Rapids, MI: Eerdmans, 1980.

Andrew Purves, *The Crucifixion of Ministry: Surrendering Our Ambitions to the Service of Christ*. Downers Grove, IL: InterVarsity Press, 2007.

John G. Stackhouse, Jr., *Partners in Christ: A Conservative Case for Egalitarianism*. Downers Grove, IL: InterVarsity Press Academic, 2010.

William H. Willimon, *Pastor: A Reader for Ordained Ministry*. Nashville, TN: Abingdon, 2002.

5

Participation: What Posture Does Christian Leadership Take?

Chapter 4 began with a cartoon-fuelled complaint about the pressure of having to be like so-and-so. But what would we prefer – the expectation that we should measure up to exemplars, or a totally blank slate in front of us? One minute we want to burn the blueprints, the next we want them badly. The whiplash is enough to make us dizzy. What are we supposed to do about this? Is there a way to appropriate best practices without turning church leadership into mimicry? In this chapter we carry on with a few more examples so as to explore the posture that church leaders should take towards the appropriation of prior experience and education, so that the following chapter can look at how church leaders prepare to tackle the practicalities of each time and place. We begin again with Moses, this time observing how he handled the recurrence of a previously conquered problem.

Moses before the rock – Numbers 17.4–6; 20.1–12

The situation Moses faces in Numbers 20 is not one you would wish on any leader: his people are stuck deep in the desert with nothing to drink and nowhere to get water. This particular stretch of desert has no corners to look around for water: it is the Desert of Zin, which means flat. To top it off this desert has just claimed Moses' sister Miriam, who had been right behind him every step of the way, and been a prominent member of the leadership team. It does not matter how much they have been through; thirst has them 'gathered together against Moses and against Aaron', second-guessing them with phrases like 'Why have you brought us here? We wish we had died at the last place!' (Num. 20.1–6).

Thankfully for Moses, he has been in this situation before. Exodus 17 has it happening way back before the encounter with Jethro, nearer the beginning of their 40-year journey. The scene then was almost exactly the same as it is in Numbers: 'The people complained against Moses' (17.3), 'Moses cried out to the Lord' (4), the Lord told Moses to 'Strike the rock, and water will come out of it, so that the people may drink' (6), and Moses did so. Fast-forward a generation and Moses is in almost the exact same situation, except it is a whole new group of people and he is more experienced now. Numbers 20 says that the people complained (Num. 20.3–5), Moses and Aaron fall on their faces before God (6), and the Lord says to take their staffs, assemble the people, and 'command the rock before their eyes to yield its water' (7–8). There is even the promise that water will come. But this time something is different. As verse 11 tells it: 'Moses lifted up his hand and struck the rock twice with his staff; water came out abundantly, and the congregation and their livestock drank.' It all sounds good – except there's a problem.

Moses and Aaron have presumed too much. They struck the rock when God had not told them to do so. This may not seem a serious matter, but it was enough to keep Moses from the Promised Land. The Lord deals Moses and Aaron the tragic blow in verse 12, saying: 'Because you did not trust in me, to show my holiness before the eyes of the Israelites, therefore you shall not bring this assembly into the land that I have given them.' What went wrong? Numbers does not relay the backstory from 40 years previous, because the reasons are simple enough: for God this striking of rock is not only a failure of trust but a diversion away from the Lord to the leadership.

So, after all that, does Moses get kept out of the Promised Land over some kind of technicality? It does seem rather harsh. But keep in mind the nature of the covenant that holds this people and their journey together. If the land they are about to walk into means anything, it is the land of promise, not possession. If the life of this people means anything, it is that they live from the power and to the glory of God alone. This *is* their blessing to the nations. To lead the people into the Promised Land and to allow them even a hint of an idea that this is theirs because they deserve it, or because of Moses' unique powers, would be to completely undermine their *modus operandi* as a people and thus their witness to the nations.

When it comes to role models and good examples, Moses has a lot to offer. But in the Bible he also serves as a cautionary tale. Moses would see but not step into the Promised Land because he and Aaron 'rebelled against my word' (Num. 27.13–14). Elsewhere God says 'both of you broke faith with me … by failing to maintain my holiness' (Deut. 32.51). By extrapolating from Exodus 17 we can make the prescience of this cautionary tale explicit. We can certainly imagine ourselves in Moses' situation, assuming that we should strike the rock like we did the first time, even convincing ourselves that God has bequeathed this gift to us and wants us to share in some of the miracle. But if God did not say to do it that way, then this would be presumptuous, even rebellious.

Does that mean we should second-guess every muscle we move in ministry, do nothing by reflex, and not rely on education and experience at all? I am not sure I would go that far, particularly given the scriptural emphasis on seeking and applying all these things diligently and faithfully. But that is the key issue isn't it? Faithfully. As Proverbs 3.5 says, 'trust in the Lord with all your heart, and do not rely on your own insight'. Whether or not Moses was relying on his rock-striking insights, or subconsciously felt he would finally get some credit by living up to his own legend, or was just getting lazy with God's words, the fact is that he repeated himself without being told, and this was not good.

Does this mean that we should *never* do the same thing twice without asking? No: It would be just as wrongheaded to make a universal principle out of this bad example as any of the good ones. But it does tell us not to make presumptions about either the ends or the means, and to attend carefully to the command of God not only as it applies to the vision but also the processes for getting there. If the example of Moses and Jethro tells us the provisional good of work-sharing and delegation, it does not mean we have licence merely to mimic them. Not only is it doubtful that the Bible even intends to be moralized in that way, but there are a number of differences between Moses' situation and ours which ought to bring a measure of nuance to any attempt to make a one-to-one application.

For instance, if we apply Jethro's advice to church life today the appropriate parallel might not be to internal role delegation but to the debate between church expansion and church planting. Moses is not assigning other tasks but sharing his own! Is Jethro's word to Moses also a word to those who would sooner maintain pastoral leadership of the hundreds and thousands rather than multiply local congregations? If the bad example of striking the rock twice for water is a cautionary tale, it should remind us to heed the commands of the living God carefully, tracing the threads of wisdom but not presuming a methodology.

All of this should give us pause over one of the most common refrains in church leadership job descriptions today, which tend to favour managerial experience and proven effectiveness over education and spiritual formation. Does this expose a reliance upon past practices (and their duplication) at the expense of being equipped to discern the Spirit in conversation with Word and Church? Consider the New Testament examples that come to mind. Would Timothy have been given a second look for many church vacancies today or would they sooner look at a guy like Simon the magician in the eighth chapter of Acts? The Samaritans considered Simon 'someone great', attributed to him 'the power of God', and had 'listened eagerly' to him 'for a long time' (Acts 8.9–10). Simon is not as outlandish a figure as some might think. In fact in another context he might carry the same name as the so-called three wise men, or magi, of Matthew 2. On another occasion his magic arts might be an issue, but that is not the problem for Acts 8. The issue is that Simon saw Peter and John laying hands on the new Samaritan believers that they might receive the Holy Spirit, and 'offered them money' so that he also could possess this power (8.18–19). He tried to 'obtain God's gift with money' (20), and in their view this was as serious as what cost Moses the Promised Land: 'You have no part or share in this, for your heart is not right before God' (21).

We are not told what becomes of Simon, because the magic is not the point. The point is that Peter and John exhort him to repent, and Simon gets the message. So chastened is he, in fact, that he does not even presume that his prayers of repentance will earn him any favour with God. The episode ends with him asking them to pray to the Lord for mercy on his behalf. From there the author of Acts whisks us away to find Philip in the wilderness with some water, teaching and baptizing another unlikely disciple, the eunuch who brought Christianity to Africa. By the time Philip is whisked away yet again we readers should get the point: like Moses before the rock, church leaders had better get used to the fact theirs is not a power to wield but a Christ to whom to yield.

No wonder Paul was willing to look back on that episode with Moses in the wilderness and say not only that the Hebrews 'drank from the spiritual rock that followed them, and that rock was Christ', but also that their punishments in the wilderness 'occurred as examples for us, so that we might not desire evil as they did' (1 Cor. 10.4–6). This should be enough for us to think twice about presuming our prior abilities and audiences should immediately carry over as assets to ministry, or that the offer of money (even in the form of state protection, as in Ezra 8.21–36) should be persuasive, or that the spiritual gifts we deploy should be considered ours to obtain and possess and to wield at will. We will return to these themes in later chapters as we consider the practicalities of church leadership more closely. For the moment let us consider one more example.

David before the people – 1 Chronicles 21.1–15; Exodus 30.12

We have already discussed how David was deemed a 'man after God's own heart' in the run-up to his kingship, as seen in his patient obedience to the Lord (1 Sam. 13.14, see Ps. 51 and Acts 13.22). But we also remember that David was not exactly a model king in every way. David's exploitation of power in adultery with Bathsheba and his insidious plot to get her husband Uriah killed on the front lines (2 Sam. 11) serve as a shocking illustration of the perils of untampered lust and inadequate accountability. No church leaders – especially the standouts – should be without moral and organizational accountability. Authority and celebrity have a way of putting even the most innocent among us into situations beyond anything we have had to handle before. A leader after God's heart is precisely *not* someone we ascertain capable of soldiering on against temptations alone, but someone who will entrust themselves to ongoing confessional relationships with God and community.

These are clear lessons for leadership to be drawn from the example of David. But there is another lesson from his leadership to which I wish to draw attention before we move on, in large part because it is so powerfully apropos but conveniently less heeded today. This is the lesson of David's unsolicited census, as told in 1 Chronicles 21.

Similar to Moses striking the rock, at first glance the scene where David calls an undue census might seem more like a petty mistake than the warrant for severe divine punishment. What happens is that David tells his army commander Joab to 'go, number Israel, from Beer-sheba to Dan, and bring me a report, so that I may know their number' (21.2). After a brief effort to talk David out of it, Joab does as he is told and reports back 1.57 million sword-wielding men in all – minus the tribes of Levi and Benjamin, whom Joab does not have the heart to count (3–6). But Joab's distaste for this whole affair is just a shadow of God's displeasure, as we find out when the Lord sends a seer to give David three options as to what kind of punishment the people of Israel will face for this sinful census (7–12). In his distress David chooses a three-day plague rather than three days of famine or three months of enemy attack, which God mercifully shortens once 70,000 persons have died (13–15). That this is but a fraction of the people (who 2 Sam. 24.1 says had already been kindling the anger of God) does not diminish the seemingly disproportionate severity of the news to our ears. Does taking an unsolicited head count really warrant such a punishment from God? Should we be stopping each time to consider this before we take attendance in church? For his part, while he was appalled at what occurred, David repented rather than protested, confessing that 'the command to count' was his and that by it he had 'sinned and done very wickedly' (17). So what was the problem?

In 1 Chronicles 23 to 27 we have a detailed accounting of the priests and the Levites and the military divisions of Israel, all of it apparently in good order at the guidance of God, so if we want to know what was so bad about this earlier census it looks like we are in similar territory to Moses and Aaron striking the rock. The problem was that this census was not only unsolicited and presumptuous on David's part, but also exhibited a lack of faith and a concern to have his own control. In 1 Chronicles 27.23 we see that even in the legitimate census of the tribes of Israel 'David did not count those below twenty years of age, for the Lord had promised to make Israel as numerous as the stars of heaven.' The implication is that unless you take a census to prepare for some constructive commission from God (such as handing the kingdom to Solomon, as per 23.1), then number-crunching the people would be an exercise in self-assurance and a testing of the promises of God.

This is underlined by reflection on Exodus 30.12, where Moses was told that 'a census of the Israelites' was to be accompanied by 'a ransom [of half a shekel to the sanctuary] for their lives to the Lord, so that no plague may come upon them for being registered'. There it was also said that 'the rich shall not give more, and the poor shall not give less', which goes to show that this was a very low tithe, ensuring that when they did count the people, everyone counted the same, and there were to be absolutely zero illusions about whose concern the numbers and the security and the promises of the people ultimately were. In God's mercy I do not think we have to imagine a plague hanging over us every time we count up our congregations or balance the books, but it would not hurt if we allowed the example of David's unsolicited census to chasten our use of numbers. Consider the resonant cautionary tale found in Acts 5. On a number of occasions in Acts it is certainly celebrated that 'the Lord added to their number those who were being saved' (2.47, see 2.41 and 5.14), but the issue the early church seemed primarily concerned with when they did their accounting was money. More specifically it was ensuring that all could be shared and that no one would fall through the cracks. That is the occasion for the aforementioned delegation of care for widows, but also for a fearful set of deaths (Acts 5–6).

In Acts 5 we see a property-owning married couple who have 'kept back some of [their] proceeds', deceived the apostles about it, and immediately fallen down and died (5.1–11). This was a community 'of one heart and soul' where 'no one claimed private ownership of any possessions, but everything they owned was held in common' (4.32) – so when this couple 'contrived' to hold back, misled the church, and lied to the apostles, their sin was against none other than God (5.4). Nothing about the story licenses any church leader to impose such a penalty on their church today, but it should certainly make us think twice about unconsciously deferring authority to the modern gods of private property, accrued wealth, and basic consumer units in the church today. Does God require this of us and why? The point in all this is not to be gripped with fear but to reckon with the giftedness of the gifts of grace, and thus in the rubric of faithfulness to learn the wisdom that begins in the fear of the Lord.

With respect to the value of examples for church leadership, where does this leave us? I think it behoves us to conclude with a reflection on the basic posture of Christian life and leadership, which brings us back to the topic of imitation (*Be like boy!*) and its long-noted tension with the notion of participation (*We like Roy!*). To erase the tension and resolve it in one direction or the other would be a problem. Imitation without participation would be religion teetering on the edge of idolatry; participation without imitation would be spirituality teetering on the edge of disobedience.

The traditional Latin phrases *imitatio Christi* and *participatio Christi* remind us that this is no abstract distinction, it is about living in accordance with Christ, not just as a historical moral figure of the past, but as resurrected Lord

of all things in the present. Earlier we took precedent for the language of imitation from such New Testament passages as Ephesians 5, 1 Corinthians 4, and
1 Thessalonians 1 and 2. If we search for the English word *participation* we might
have a harder time, but that is because one of the more relevant words is the
Greek *koinonia*, which is more often than not translated in terms of fellowship,
sharing, and partnership. None of these are bad translations, but we do tend
to treat them as secondary, supportive supplements to our individual moral
choices. Such oppositional rhetoric is uncalled for, however. The truth of the
matter is that *imitatio* and *participatio* are not opposed but complementary; they
are ultimately reconciled in Christ.

A full survey of *koinonia* and *in Christ* texts would be wonderful, but for our
purposes it suffices to draw out this point simply by pressing further into the
imitation texts to which we have already referred. In 1 Thessalonians 1 and 2
we recall that the church in Thessalonica was praised for imitating the church
in Judea (2.14), and that the believers' imitation of the apostles made them in
turn an example to all (1.6–7) – but what was praised was that they 'turned to
God from idols, to serve a [God who is] living and true' (1.9). In 1 Corinthians
4.16 we recall that Paul said, 'be imitators of me' – but the issue at stake was his
'ways in Christ Jesus', which were not a matter of boastful talk or heroism, but
only the power of the Spirit as could be seen in Timothy his 'faithful child in the
Lord' (4.16–20). And in Ephesians 5.1 we heard the call to 'be imitators of God'
– but this meant 'being rooted and grounded in love', and having the 'power to
comprehend [it], with all the saints' (3.17–18). The *imitatio Christi* which thus
proceeds is where each is 'given grace according to the measure of Christ's gift'
through the Spirit in the body of Christ (4.6–13).

Clearly there is a place for heeding good (and bad) examples, finding role
models, pursuing education, and crafting competencies to the service and glory
of God, but this is our participation with the saints in the things of God, not just
preparation until we can go it alone. If imitation becomes the definitive mode
of Christian life and leadership, we may be on the road of idolatry rather than
that of a living Lord. As Andrew Purves put it in his 2004 book, *Reconstructing
Pastoral Theology: A Christological Foundation*:

> Of course, a pastor must develop interpersonal skills and understand emo-
> tions, human development, and the complexities of human relationships and
> family systems. But none of these supplies the ground, the basic content, that

gives pastoral work its specific identity as Christian … [Having] an imitative rather than … a participatory approach to ministry … builds on a reductionist Christology that limits Jesus to a moral influence because it finds no place for … his vicarious humanity and continuing priesthood. The effect [of which] is to cast the pastor back upon his or her own resources … [in] a ministry by works rather than a ministry through grace … [that leads effectively to Jesus'] replacement by an ethical Christ-principle separated from him. (pp. xxix–xxx)

For all the good there may be in recreating experiences or planning intentionally, the posture of Christian leadership must essentially remain a matter of participating in Christ's ongoing work by grace, rather than measured masterplans of effectiveness.

Part of God's great provision for us, of course, is that we have examples in the communion of saints that we can follow and learn from, both for their wise moves and their bad mistakes. But for all that can be said about their examples, what we are mainly meant to notice about that 'great cloud of witnesses' is their *faith* (Heb. 12.1). Furthermore all of it – from Abel to Abraham, Moses to Barak, and 'David and Samuel and the prophets' (Heb. 11.4–32) – is bound up in this startling conclusion:

Yet all these, though they were commended for their faith, did not receive what was promised, since God had provided something better so that they would not, without us, be made perfect. (11.39–40)

If that does not chasten our assumption that we can judge good leaders based on whether we see immediate results from their work, I do not know what does. Even the efforts of Moses are yet incomplete, waiting to be added to ours in the perfect work of God.

It should thus be both humbling and comforting for us to know that neither our apparent successes nor our apparent failures to measure up are ever the end of the story. So take heart from the examples of leaders in the Bible who, if they have anything to show us, have shown us that 'the Lord does not see as mortals see; they look on the outward appearance, but the Lord looks on the heart' (1 Sam. 16.7). For all his successes and all his failings, what made David 'a man after God's own heart' (13.14) was most manifest in his confession that 'a broken and contrite heart, O God, you will not despise' (Ps. 51.17); and what Paul reflected on as most relevant about David's selection as king was that God said he would 'carry out all my wishes' (Acts 13.22). The fundamental posture of a Christian leader is thus one of penitent obedience to God. That is, faithfulness before effectiveness; effectiveness in service of faithfulness.

The placement of *imitatio Christi* under the primary posture of *participatio Christi* recalls us to the fact that ours is a joined effort proceeding not from individually appropriated laws but ever anew from the grace that we share in Christ. Models and examples are wisely to be heeded, but the stories of the Bible are disrespected if they are reduced to moralistic aphorisms or self-help principles for living. For every leadership principle that can be found in the Bible there appears to be a warning against simply reproducing it. That is because they are words to the wise, not models for our mastery. If we do not learn from our biblical role models that the decisive issue is obeying God under the guidance of Word and Spirit, then we may not yet have learned from them at all. If we think of participation with Christ as a shared rather than an individualistic endeavour, then we have reason to get educated and experienced in the fields where God calls us to work, even as it keeps us from banking on it. There is a threat of idolatry in both the presumptions of intuition and in the preparedness of institution. With these extended reflections on the posture of church leadership and the examples of scripture, we turn in our next chapter to the definition of three habits at the heart of an attentive leader's life.

Further reflection

Read Hebrews 11 and go back over the stories of one of the figures mentioned there. List the examples they offer, then put a P beside those that speak of participation, and an I beside those that offer wisdom for imitation.

Think of a Christian whose leadership or spirituality you admire. Make a list of the things you would like to imitate, and also list the hints which point to their dependence upon the strength and guidance of God.

What tendencies or presumptions of modern leadership do you think about when you reflect on the metaphor of Moses striking rock, or David calling a census? What personal tendencies come to mind? Pray to submit these to God.

Further reading

J. Todd Billings, *Union with Christ: Reframing Theology and Ministry for the Church*. Grand Rapids, MI: Baker Academic, 2011.

Michael J. Gorman, *Becoming the Gospel: Paul, Participation, and Mission*. Grand Rapids, MI: Eerdmans, 2015.

Elizabeth A. Johnson, *Truly our Sister: A Theology of Mary in the Communion of Saints*. London: Continuum, 2003.

Justin Lewis-Anthony, *If You Meet George Herbert on the Road, Kill Him: Radically Re-thinking Priestly Ministry*. London: Mowbray, 2009.

Eugene H. Peterson, *Under the Unpredictable Plant: An Exploration in Vocational Holiness*. Grand Rapids, MI: Eerdmans, 1992.

Andrew Purves, *Reconstructing Pastoral Theology: A Christological Foundation*. Louisville, KY: Westminster John Knox, 2004.

John Webster, *Holiness*. London: SCM, 2003.

6

Rhythms: What Habits Are at the Heart of Christian Leadership?

The first half of this book has been about identifying what makes church leadership go around. One could turn to all kinds of metaphors for the sensibility of coming to grips with the vital practices of Christian leadership, but one could do worse than the metaphor of the heart. Getting to the heart of a matter is about identifying the centrally organic pattern of activity that keeps the life-blood pumping through something. The heart of the matter is not just a thing but a pattern of activity. There can be all kinds of bodies attached to it, but the heart still needs to beat. It does not do the living for you, but you do not live without it. Church leaders will differ from each other in many ways, but if we identify the habits at the heart of church leadership we are talking about rhythms of life that go with the territory no matter what.

Like the heart, these practices tend to go unseen unless you go looking for them. The social pressure to perform and the temptation to self-reliance often conspire to make these practices the first to go from a routine. But the church body that sets to work without its heart will eventually be tossed around like a rag doll, or deployed like Frankenstein's monster. I am not claiming to be good at these things or even naturally inclined towards them, but everywhere I turn it is affirmed to me that these are worth keeping up. There is nothing automatic about them, but they are practices that God has invested with the promise of the Holy Spirit. They are not life itself, but are the gracious rhythms of Christian life, given for our participation.

The most quoted proverb in church leadership is probably 'where there is no vision, the people perish'. Often this King James Version of Proverbs 29.18 is quoted to underline a vision statement or a set of values or goals, but other translations run similar to the New Revised Standard Version, which alternatively says: 'Where there is no prophecy, the people cast off restraint.' In that case the point is that unless we are perpetually guided by the living Word of God, we are setting ourselves adrift. The second half of the verse says 'happy are those who keep the law'. We are a far cry from the typical motivational poster about vision casting. That is not to say there is no place for such things, but we also recall Proverbs 19.21: 'The human mind may devise many plans, but it is the purpose of the Lord that will be established.' As Dietrich Bonhoeffer warned so vividly in *Life Together*, the Christian community 'is not an ideal which we must realize; it is rather a reality created by God in which we may participate' (p. 18). One 'who loves [their] dream of a community more than the Christian community itself becomes a destroyer of the latter,' no matter how 'earnest and sacrificial' the intent (pp. 15–16).

Remembering that God originally preferred to lead through prophets rather than kings, we recognize that God works with various organization structures and individuals but prefers to stick to that basic mode, which is to lead us with the living Word. Pacemakers may have their place in medicine, but there is no reinventing the heart of Christian life and ministry. The rhythms of life that govern church life and leadership remain constant through the ages. When we feel stifled by our church experience or have a flare for the over-creative, it is precisely then that we must find the pulse again. It is not without but *within* these divinely sanctioned rhythms of life that churches flourish in beautifully diverse ways across languages, cultures, and sanctified imaginations.

Rather than get too clever for my own good, then, I want to gather together the theological threads and spiritual–ethical insights of a number of key Christian texts from the last few decades so that we can trace a threefold pattern of church life and leadership that is found within them. My hope is that as we hold up our stethoscope we will hear the church's heartbeat and get caught up in its rhythms of life as leaders. For a guide to recognizing this threefold pattern I invite you to see Table 1 below, called 'Life rhythms of church leaders'. There you will see reference to the resources that have influenced my thinking in this regard, not by their ingenuity so much as their clarity of insight into the vital habits that have remained constant through the ages. The books I am drawing from are Henri

Nouwen's *In the Name of Jesus: Reflections on Church Leadership*, and Eugene Peterson's *Working the Angles: The Shape of Pastoral Integrity*, but I will also link up with Stanley Hauerwas's *The Peaceable Kingdom: A Primer in Christian Ethics*, and Gordon T. Smith's *Evangelical, Sacramental and Pentecostal: Why the Church Should Be All Three*. The table aligns all this with the grammars of theology and prayer.

Table 1: Life rhythms of church leaders

	1 – Prayer	*2 – Fellowship*	*3 – Scripture*
Temptation (Matt. 4)	Relevance *'command these stones'*	Spectacle *'throw yourself down'*	Power *'all these I will give you'*
Challenge (John 21)	Love of God *'do you love me?'*	Life Together *'feed my sheep'*	Cruciform Service *'someone will take you'*
Discipline (Nouwen)	Contemplative Prayer	Confession and Forgiveness	Theological Reflection
Pastoral Act (Peterson)	Praying *'bring before God'*	Spiritual Direction	Reading Scripture
Mark of Church (Hauerwas)	Sacraments *'our fervent prayers'*	Mutual Upbuilding and Correction	Word Preached and Heard
Dimension of Grace (Smith)	Sacramental	Pentecostal	Evangelical
Ministry of Christ	High Priest	Shepherd King	Gospel Prophet
Divine Orientation	Father God	Holy Spirit	Son Jesus

1 – Prayer

Henri Nouwen's moving portrait of leadership *In the Name of Jesus* is divided into three sections which each begin with a reflection on Jesus' post-baptismal temptations in the wilderness, move to a reflection on his resurrection appearance to Peter, and then extrapolate from this the proposal of a vital discipline for Christian leadership. The first section begins with a reflection on the temptation to 'command these stones to become loaves of bread' (Matt. 4.3). Nouwen describes this in modern terms as the temptation 'to be relevant' (p. 15), which is to turn from the good impulse of *caring* to a self-centred fixation on *accomplishment*. Jesus does not deny the importance of bread-sharing, but resists the temptation to 'live by bread alone', signalling that we are not called to prove ourselves according to how effectively we meet the felt needs of society (however legitimate), but to live and serve 'by every word that comes from the mouth of God' (4.4). This is not to say that we do not do good things to meet real needs, rather to insist that we do them as God tells us to, not in self-directed altruism. This is resonant with contemporary reflections on the deleterious effects of philanthropic aid from a safe distance.

Nouwen saw a corrective to this do-goodery not only in Jesus' resistance to temptation but also in his post-resurrection reinstatement and commissioning of Peter. After Peter had thrice denied him at death's door, the risen Jesus asked Peter three times 'do you love me?' Nouwen considered this to be not just a poetic echo but the establishment of a clear precedent for the rest of this rock of the church's life. Above all it would be intimately prayerful.

> [F]or the future of Christian leadership it is of vital importance to reclaim the mystical aspect of theology so that every word spoken, every advice given, and every strategy developed can come from a heart that knows God intimately … Through the discipline of contemplative prayer, Christian leaders have to learn to listen again and again to the voice of love and to find there the wisdom and courage to address whatever issue presents itself to them. (p. 30)

If you feel instantly pigeon-holed by this onto the emotional–experiential end of a spectrum where your personality does not belong, then it is important to clarify that it is not the case that 'intimate', 'contemplative' and 'mystical' are reducible to descriptions of an emotional or a sentimental state. Though it may come easier to some than others, prayerfulness is not reducible to a personality trait. Though it includes our emotions, love is not reducible to a feeling. Though it is helped by slowing down, contemplation is not reducible to mindfulness. Contemplative prayer is prayer that puts the whole self regularly at God's service, heart, mind, soul, and strength. No one part of the human self is going to corner the market on what that means. Prayer is the essential first discipline of church leadership because we hang on God's every word like people caught up in the love between God and each and every part of God's creation.

Eugene Peterson's *Working the Angles* similarly identifies prayer as the first of three 'pastoral acts' or 'angles' that 'are so basic, so critical, that they determine the shape of everything else' (p. 3). Church leadership is like a triangle: it can be all kinds of colours and sizes as long as it has three angles that add up to 180 degrees. Like Nouwen, Peterson starts with prayer because prayer is so easily the first to go.

> It is nice to be needed. More than nice: it is downright flattering … The edge began to wear off of the flattery when I realized that among the considerable demands on my time not one demanded that I practice a life of prayer. And yet prayer was at the very heart of the vocation I had entered … We need a strategy that takes into account the daily dilemma of living between these two sets of demands that seem to cancel each other out … The first set of demands is that we respond with compassionate attentiveness to the demands of the people around us … The second set of demands is that we respond with fervent prayer to the demand of God for our attention, to listen … and not bluff our way through by adopting a professionalized role. (pp. 64–5)

Making prayer a regular part of one's life obviously requires finding some kind of personalized rhythm. There are all kinds of ways to do this. Daily, weekly, and seasonally habituated, prayer does not need to be exciting or excruciating, eloquent or ecstatic, energizing or even effective – it just needs to happen. It can be cheerful or melancholy, pensive or emotional, alone or in a crowd, loosely structured or liturgical. The verbose may be disciplined by Psalms, the lost for words may find them in the rubric of the Lord's Prayer. The resources to help with this are endless – so much so that we can easily get carried away with techniques and gimmicks, or pressured into measuring ourselves next to the powerful experiences and relatable anecdotes of others. But the point is not any of these modes or results of contemplative prayer, but the rhythm of actually doing it. Prayer finds its language and patterns in the Bible, particularly in the Psalms, because prayer is not based on our own piety or flowery speech, but is a dialogue with the one conversation partner who always has both the first word and the last (pp. 43–7).

There is a good deal of continuity between these spiritual disciplines and the classic Marks of a Church. Our prayers are personally framed and publicly shaped in Sacrament. As Stanley Hauerwas puts it in *The Peaceable Kingdom*, 'baptism and eucharist are our most fervent prayers and set the standard for all of our other prayers … [I]t is through prayer that we learn to make ourselves open to God's presence' (p. 108). The sacraments are the embodied social acts that frame and fuel the daily habit of praying our Lord's Prayer after him, which always begins 'Our Father', whether we pray it in private or not. In prayer we worship God and accept that we do so along with everyone else, whether we like them or not. These prayers and prayerful acts are not just personal piety but the core of an alternative social ethic as potentially dangerous as what got Daniel put in the lion's den. As Hauerwas writes: 'These are the essential rituals of our politics. Through them we learn who we are. Instead of being motives or causes for effective social work … these liturgies *are* our effective … social witness' (p. 108). Gordon Smith's *Evangelical, Sacramental and Pentecostal* points out that the sacraments begin and end with what's called *epiclesis*, that is, with the prayer for the Holy Spirit to use them and make them real (p. 92). At the heart of *epiclesis* is the confession that these acts are not *our* acts but acts of God. As such the sacramental life speaks to the corporate embodiment of that basic act of the church's life, which pivots entirely on the regular submission of heart, mind, soul, and body to God in love, which is then turned to love of neighbour. In an important respect, church just *is* prayer, and so church leadership cannot live without it.

2 – Fellowship

The second section of Henri Nouwen's leadership book is about moving 'from popularity to ministry', as inspired by Jesus' resistance to the temptation to put the power of God on display by jumping from the temple and having the angels catch him (Matt. 4.6). For Nouwen, this is the temptation 'to be spectacular'.

Put this way it may seem ridiculous, but who has not wished for one more sign that God is really with us? Who has not wished for a visible vindication of one's ministry? In the face of this desire Jesus insists that one does not put God to the test, and references the very Scriptures being twisted to tempt him otherwise. As Nouwen puts it, 'Jesus refused to be a stuntman. He did not come to prove himself,' because Jesus did not need 'to demonstrate that he had something worthwhile to say' (p. 38). In other words, the work of God in Christ is good in itself. To measure it by some other good would undermine it completely. This is what lies behind Jesus' thrice-repeated re-commissioning of Peter on the beach. We can imagine Peter would have been desperate to prove himself to Jesus, to have some kind of special assignment to reverse the course of his denials and get him back on track as the 'rock' on which the church would be built. But John 21 tells us that each time Jesus asked Peter about his love he simply reiterated *ad nauseam* that the proper response is to feed Jesus' sheep (21.15–17). The lesson here, for Nouwen, is that one does not lead a Christian community by figuring out an end product and then administering a utilitarian procedure for getting there. We apply ourselves to following Christ faithfully; we do not apply Christ to some predetermined standard of functionality.

Unfortunately, there are countless pressures working against this. The obvious one is outright rebellion against Jesus, but the more insidious one occurs when we are victims of our own success, or of our need to appear successful. Church leaders are particularly susceptible in this regard. The pressure to be heroic and persuasive gives us the impression that we had better not let anyone see us crack. By taking our cues from the entertainment and service industries, we have somehow convinced ourselves to stand at a safe distance and model ourselves on the movers and shakers of this world (p. 43–5). For Nouwen this opens up a devastating downward spiral. 'Often I have the impression that priests and ministers are the least-confessing people in the Christian community', he observes, but when they

> live their ministry mostly in their heads and relate the Gospel as a set of valuable ideas to be announced, the body quickly takes revenge by screaming loudly for affection and intimacy. Christian leaders are called to live … in the body – not only in their own bodies, but also in the corporate body of the community, and to discover there the presence of the Holy Spirit. Confession and forgiveness are precisely the disciplines by which … the dark powers

are taken out of their carnal isolation, … disarmed and dispelled and a new integration between body and spirit is made possible. (pp. 48–9)

In other words: the world asks for proof; Jesus asks for followers. The world asks for superheroes; Jesus asks for shepherds. To be more precise, Jesus asks for under-shepherds who are themselves counted among the sheep. The basic habit this implies is described by Nouwen as the discipline of confession and forgiveness.

Establishing a rhythm of confession and forgiveness does not entail the repetitious recitation of a laundry list of sinful faux pas to someone who smothers it in a blanket of amnesty. This is about relationships that bring all of life before God in the context of Christ-sustained communion. Nouwen thinks this confessional life is vital not only to the health of the church being led, but to the spiritual, emotional, relational, and physical health of the leader. Church leaders cannot be expected to be in close intimate relationship with each person they serve (this would require another sort of heroism), but they must be established in the very patterns of mutuality that are at the heart of the community they lead. This means taking part in the fellowship more broadly, and also ensuring that one has in one's life a handful of what might be called *confessors*. This role is not reserved only for priests in a confessional booth; it is part of the priesthood of believers to one another in the rhythms of Christian fellowship. In a general sense this is as straightforward as making open and authentic friendships a real part of your life as a leader. In a specific sense it is about attending to what makes such friendships uniquely Christian, and tunes them to the particular demands of one's vocation. For church leaders, such confessional relationships need be geared to the particular confidences and pressures of such a life.

The 'pastoral act' Peterson names at this angle of the church leader's life is 'spiritual direction'. As he explains it, 'spiritual direction takes place when two people agree to give their full attention to what God is doing in one (or both) of their lives and seek to respond in faith' (p. 150). This discipline goes by other names as well. 'Accountability partners', 'prayer triplets', and 'spiritual friendships' tend to be the names given to those confessional relationships that are sought among peers. 'Coaches', 'mentors', and 'spiritual directors' tend to be relationships wherein one party is given the right to ask the questions and offer counsel in an intentionally directed way. Like many, I have found formal mentors harder to find, but have stumbled into friendships and accountable ministry relationships which convince me that these are worth seeking out and making intentional rather than leaving to chance. I do not know how I would survive in church leadership, or life generally, without timely moments of spiritual direction and solidarity provided by colleagues, Christian friends, mentors, or partners in ministry. We need to ensure that genuine Christ-confessing conversations are a regular rhythm of our lives, generally, and our vocations, specifically.

This is the leader's participation in the mark of a church known as 'church discipline'. Unfortunately when people think of church discipline they tend to think of heavy-handed disciplinary processes that lead to excommunication. This is because of the worst case scenario that results when, as per Jesus' instructions in Matthew 18, a person has been confronted directly and discreetly about some moral offence but has been unrepentant, thereby effectively refusing to be reconciled to the church. Rather than surrender this mark of a church to its own worst caricature, however, we ought to recognize it as a constructive communal practice (or 'discipline') of genuine spiritual and moral accountability, hinging not on anyone's moral perfection but on real-time confessions of Jesus as Lord. 'Church discipline' is better known as reciprocal spiritual direction, the ministry of reconciliation, or, as Hauerwas refers to it in *The Peaceable Kingdom*, as 'mutual upbuilding and correction' (p. 109). It is a social ethic whereby we learn 'to live in the presence of others without fear and envy' and in this way witness to the humanity-renewing fellowship of the Holy Spirit (p. 110).

Along with Gordon Smith we might reckon this vitality of spiritual connectivity to be a particular contribution of the Pentecostal stream to the wholeness of the ecumenical church (see Chapter 6). However, where Pentecostalism tends to emphasize the 'immediacy' and intimacy of *personal* experiences of the Spirit, here we follow the Spirit through to its proper conclusion, which is to bring people into loving communion together with Christ the reconciler and Shepherd King. For that reason I would rather think of this 'dimension of grace' as *Charismatic* – not in the sense of experientialism but in its fuller biblical sense as a fellowship of gift-sharing of believers who are diversely 'graced' to build one another up in Christ. In Chapter 8 we will see how popular modern notions of 'charisma' actually bring us back to Henri Nouwen's original concern with the temptations of ministry. If Christian leadership is about persuasiveness, dynamism, or charm rather than the particular spiritual gift of leadership to the body of Christ, then it may well be flat-lining the church right when hearts are felt to be racing. This is not to say that spirituality does not include the spectacular, but is to say that the discipline of accountable fellowship is the healthy habit at the beating heart of the church between its unexpected highs.

3 – Scripture

The third section of Henri Nouwen's *In the Name of Jesus: Reflections on Christian Leadership* discusses the shift 'from leading to being led', which is obviously rather counter-intuitive. Given that we discussed this in one way or another in Chapters 2 and 5, it should be fairly clear by now what I take it to mean, but the discipline that Nouwen hinges it on is possibly rather surprising. The insistence that leaders be led by God would perhaps suggest the habits of contemplative prayer or spiritual direction, but what Nouwen directs our attention to in this case is the discipline of 'theological reflection'. The temptation he begins with is the one where Jesus is taken up a mountain to look out over the nations in all their splendour, and is offered charge over all of them in an instant if he will give the devil one small moment of worship (Matt. 4.8–9). It is, as Nouwen says, the temptation 'to be powerful' (p. 55) – a temptation that is at its greatest when we are most convinced of the goodness of our intentions.

Jesus' resistance to this temptation is not only predicated on the Great Commandment (Deut. 6.13) but for Nouwen is also reflected in his resurrection reinstatement of Peter.

On the beach Jesus tells Peter that if he loves him and feeds his sheep, it is liable to get him killed:

'Very truly, I tell you, when you were younger, you used to fasten your own belt and to go wherever you wished. But when you grow old, you will stretch out your hands, and someone else will fasten a belt around you and take you where you do not wish to go.' (He said this to indicate the kind of death by which he would glorify God.) After this he said to him, 'Follow me.' (John 21.18–19)

It would be hard to think of a stronger contrast to that desert temptation, which offered an easy win by way of a mere transference of power. Jesus reveals to us in both his resistance to temptation and in his charge to Peter that the restoration of creation would not be accomplished by the perpetuation of that original sin, but by the good and proper impulses of creaturely flourishing: namely, by submission to the Creator.

Whether or not Jesus knew this intuitively by virtue of his divinity, when he resisted the temptation to bow down for power he referred to the revelation of God in scripture, which specifically forbids such bowing in any circumstances whatsoever. Thus for Jesus to later say 'follow me' is one of the loudest declarations of his own divinity imaginable, but the most startling part is that following him requires a preference for death rather than life by some other means. To submit to God within a rebellious creation will mean going against the grain of self interest in order to go with God. The promise of new creation is a call to faith, and people of faith will be willing to die for it. Not every church leader will be martyred, but non-violent martyrs are symbols to us of what being a Christian looks like in this world if we follow through on the logic of our baptism in the run of our daily lives in a violently selfish world.

So church leaders resist the temptation to power. But is this not frankly oxymoronic? How does one both lead and revoke power? Technically speaking I used power just to pull myself out of bed this morning, not to mention when on the morning commute I put my left indicator light on and declared to trailing cars my right of way. Similarly, for Christian communities that submit themselves together to the lead of God, there is a 'right of way' granted to one another to serve in the responsibilities God assigns according to the gifts God provides. Any exercise of leadership or authority is itself submitted to Christ and to the community in accord with its commissioned authorization under the guidance of the Spirit, all held accountable under the authority of the Scriptures as received by the church. In other words, the church leader is a follower submitting a service to God and to the community – and the church leader would rather die than forsake service for power. As Nouwen put it:

> The way of the Christian leader is not the way of upward mobility in which our world has invested so much, but the way of downward mobility ending on the cross ... I, obviously, am not speaking about a psychologically weak leadership in which the Christian leader is simply the passive victim of the manipulations of his milieu ... What, then, is the discipline required of a leader who can live with outstretched hands? I propose here the discipline of ... strenuous theological reflection [which] will allow us to discern critically where we are being led. (pp. 62–5)

Thus no matter how tempting it is to take shortcuts to effective ministry, the church leader remains theologically reflective in action, and active in theological reflection.

Eugene Peterson makes this point by pointing out that scripture is God speaking to us, and that speech is something you listen to, not something you read. That is not to say that written works of scripture and theology cannot be a means of God's self-revelation; rather, it is to underline the primary place of holy scripture as a mode of divine speech, itself bearing witness to the Word of God, Jesus Christ. It is the means by which the Spirit speaks to the churches (Rev. 1–3). Without this the Bible is just a good book at best, or an idol at worst. Without the Bible, the same can be said for group-think or the individual conscience. 'In listening the speaker is in charge; in reading the reader is in charge', writes Peterson, but:

> The intent in reading Scripture, among people of faith, is to extend the range of our listening to the God who reveals himself in word, to become acquainted with the ways in which he has spoken in various times and places, along with the ways in which people respond when he speaks. (p. 89)

What is needed now, as ever, is church leaders who believe the Spirit is speaking to the churches with the Word. We might prefer a God who simply has one-to-one conversations with each of us in isolation, such as we might have had if the resurrected Jesus had not ascended to heaven but had stayed on earth to travel door to door. But God's preferred mode has been for Christ to reign from heaven and to be present on earth where two or three are gathered to be reconciled, to celebrate the sacraments, and to hear the Word. The Spirit does of course speak to individuals, but the main way God speaks to and in the world today is in and through churches. We go to the Holy Scriptures together in the fellowship of the Spirit, to hear the Word from God for all time and to hear the Spirit guiding us into truth for today.

Thus whether a church leader is a teacher and a preacher or not, the personal discipline of time spent in scripture is simply necessary. It does not require constant epiphanies, it just requires our care and attention. If reading is not a church leader's strong suit, there is going to have to be some other means for digesting the words of Scripture like manna from heaven. For most church leaders however, reading (and writing) are going to be fairly standard requirements. Literacy is not required to be a Christian, of course, but reading has been the provision of God by which the Scriptures are passed on and turned into speech across space and time. This has been so since the birth of the church, but as time has gone on we have become more and more dependent on the written word for the transmission of Scripture and for its understanding and sharing across generations and across the globe. This may seem onerous, but good things tend to involve effort and concentration. To be a church leader of any kind is going to mean spending time in study, becoming equipped to handle the Word of God, and in fact being formed in the reading of it. Depending on the responsibilities and requirements of the church leadership position in question, this may mean years of sacrifice and study. Short cuts only pay off in the short run. A solid stretch of time studying the Word of God along with and at the centre of other relevant disciplines is a must for any prospective full time church leader.

Many times the Scriptures will feel unproductive and dry, but just like everything else, the Scriptures are not measured by their immediate felt results. It can be a good sign if we are not always thrilled by what we find. Like Peterson said, reading can be a means of personal dominance and control, and so can be a dangerous way of projecting onto the Word of God what we want to confirm. Worse, it can then become a way of justifying the projection of such ideas onto others. But when it is where we go with the church to listen for the Word in the Spirit, accountable to and focused on the local church with which we commune – there is really nothing quite like it. The Scriptures are provided by God through the use of hundreds of thousands of Christians working together to pass on the apostles' and prophets' teaching, share interpretations, hone understanding, and learn to communicate and live the ways and works of God. Church leaders are a part of that conversation, whether they preach or not, because being part of that conversation is what it means to be a church.

The other name Peterson has for reading scripture is 'contemplative exegesis', which brings us right back around to Nouwen's first discipline, contemplative prayer, and shows how interconnected these are. Just as the Scriptures inform our prayers, so too is prayer our approach to scripture. To do exegesis means literally 'to lead' (*geisthai*) 'out of' (*exe-*) the text. Making theological reflection a rhythm of life requires not only study but simply reading the Bible to hear it; to hear God – no strings attached. There is no pressure of having something to show for it. This is why 'personal devotions' are often separated from 'bible study' or 'sermon prep', so that our times of Bible intake are not just utilitarian, driven to some project. It is not necessary to be overly legalistic about this, however, let alone to fall for the strange misconception that reading to study or teach is somehow unspiritual. People sometimes say that systematic study puts God in a box, but it is just as easy to do this with 'devotional' reading. In truth, careful theological study is a concerted practice of disciplining ourselves to be interrupted by God and to hear God on God's own terms, rather than rushing to our own conclusions. One of the paradoxes of Bible study is that the more you master it the less its master you are. It is what Jesus would have been gesturing toward when he was tempted to misuse scripture for his own purposes, and answered with more scripture: 'It is written, "One does not live by bread alone, but by every word that comes from the mouth of God"' (Matt. 4.4; see Deut. 8.3). It is better to make this happen regularly than to insist on certain ways it has to be done. The point is to make it part of your life until you find the life that is in it.

The central place where the church attends to the Scriptures is in the sermon, which is the Mark of a Church in which the people are gathered to hear the Word of God, as the Spirit guides them in the hearing of its proclamation and explanation by someone commissioned to lead the task. As Hauerwas explains it in *The Peaceable Kingdom*, this is a key aspect of the church's social ethic: it is 'through the preaching of God's good news and our willingness to hear it that we become a people of witness. Preaching is not just the telling; it is also the hearing' (p. 108). We see this from day one of the church's existence. When the Spirit of the ascended Christ descended on the first believers they caused a scene by their declaration of the wonders of God in the languages of the world, and then heard the first sermon, and then celebrated baptisms, and then 'devoted themselves to the apostles' teaching and fellowship, to the breaking of bread and the prayers' (Acts 2.42). Church is the perpetuation of that event. The Word taught and preached, heard and obeyed, has been at the heartbeat of the church since the events of Pentecost and Emmaus, and extended well before that in the DNA of the people of God through the Law and the Prophets, albeit in a different form. This is a hearing act as much as it is a speaking act. The preachers listen and then gather the congregation to hear together. Ideally this is not the end of it. The hearing of God's Word ripples forward and is a vital part of the church's decision-making processes, prayer and small groups, confessional lives, and mission work. Why? Because this is how we follow God's lead. None of us in control. We each have our gifts and tasks in the assembly of people who are gathered to receive and be guided by the living Word of God. As Stephen

Fowl and Gregory Jones explain in their excellent little book *Reading in Communion*: 'No particular community of believers can be sure of what a faithful interpretation of Scripture will entail in any specific situation until it actually engages in the hard process of conversation, argument, discussion, prayer and practice' (p. 20). This is an integral part of their whole live together, ideally not in a cumbersome but a seamlessly life-giving way.

This aspect of the church's existence has become the particular focus of the Protestant tradition, and in particular its Evangelical stream, but theirs is not a monopoly on it. Nor should it be. As Smith explains in *Evangelical, Sacramental & Pentecostal*, each of these aspects of the church's life need each other: Bible readers need the 'sacramental corrective to biblicism' (p. 67) which is the name for what we do when we divorce the text of the Bible from the living Word Jesus, put it at our own disposal and set up our methods and interpretations as our sacred cow. By the sacraments we die to self and live to Christ, accepting the whole church as co-readers of Scripture in the process. In this way both Word and Sacrament are also correctives to individualism, just as the Pentecostal stream offers a corrective to ritualism. Each of these three marks of a church is important – Word, Sacrament, and the Fellowship of the Spirit – and each is a vital rhythm of a church leader's life. Together these life rhythms complement each other for our good, not by some self-help strategy where we use them like a set of checks and balances in a system of our own devising, but because they come together in the economy of God's merciful work with us, in us, and through us to the world. These are the sinews that hold the Body of Christ together, and which present it as witness to the world. These are the acts in which Christ has promised to be present on earth each day till the end of time. To be a church leader is to be personally caught up in them, and then to discharge one's responsibilities within the church's combined efforts in that regard as well.

This brings us to the end of the chapter on the habits of a church leader, the section on vital practices, and indeed the halfway point of the book. As we turn further into pragmatic realities, we recall that whatever we might say about excellence in certain skills, the acquisition of practical wisdom, and the development of appropriate habits, at the core of it all stands the confession that Christian leadership is about following the lead of God. This is so not only until you are ready to take off the training wheels, but on and on with every pedal. If we are suspicious of following role models and tradition, we should be equally suspicious of following uninformed intuitions and inattentive assumptions of status quo. If we look at the wisdom literature of the Old Testament we see that wisdom begins with fear of the Lord (Prov. 9.10) and carries on with it all the same – even and especially as we gather confidence with experience and advice from those before and around us. If the attention that has been paid so far upon such things as basic habits and the marks of a church feels constricting, I hope the second half of the book will show how these things begin to play out even in the most taken for granted of leadership practicalities. Far from being a wet blanket thrown over the fires of creativity, I have actually found the basics of church life and leadership to be like fuel for the sanctified imagination. Those who feel constricted by them might do well to ask themselves: Have we really considered how our current needs and ideas might be reconciled with the vital practices of Christian life and community? What happens if we put contemporary pragmatics *together* with the received theological wisdom? More often than not I have found that what seems at first to be an impractical theological obstacle actually just turns out to be a gridlock on the imagination that a community gathered prayerfully to discern the direction of Word and Spirit will in time find opened up in exciting ways. Sometimes from these new horizons we can look back on our prior premises and practices and realize that we had not interpreted them or implemented them in ways that were everything God intended for them. The practices of prayer, theological reflection, and mutual discipleship are thus the beating heart of church life and leadership, no matter what practical out-workings they fuel.

Further reflection

Of the three basic habits covered in this chapter, which has fitted into your life most easily, and which has been the hardest to keep up or feel good about?

Do the three temptations named ring true to you? Which is most tempting for you? Can you think of the good side of each? What good thing is each one a shadow of?

Make three columns on a page, one for each life rhythm, and list what is important about each, first as it relates to your life, then to church, then to its witness in society. Then list practical things you might do to embed these into your life. Be realistic.

Further reading

Karl Barth, *Evangelical Theology: An Introduction*, trans. G. Foley. Grand Rapids, MI: Eerdmans, 1963.

Dietrich Bonhoeffer, *Life Together*, trans. J.W. Doberstein. London: SCM, 1954.

Dietrich Bonhoeffer, *Spiritual Care*, trans. J.C. Rochelle. Minneapolis, MN: Fortress, 1985.

Stephen E. Fowl and L. Gregory Jones, *Reading in Communion: Scripture and Ethics in Christian Life*. Eugene, OR: Wipf and Stock, 1998.

Stanley Hauerwas, *The Peaceable Kingdom: A Primer in Christian Ethics*. London: SCM, 1983.

Wesley Hill, *Washed and Waiting: Reflections on Christian Faithfulness and Homosexuality*. Grand Rapids, MI: Zondervan, 2010.

Sunder Krishan, *The Conquest of Inner Space: Learning the Language of Prayer*. Toronto: Scarlet Cord Press, 2003.

Henri Nouwen, *In the Name of Jesus: Reflections on Christian Leadership*. New York: Crossroad, 1989.

Eugene H. Peterson, *Working the Angles: The Shape of Pastoral Integrity*. Grand Rapids, MI: Eerdmans, 1987.

Andrew Purves, *The Resurrection of Ministry: Serving in the Hope of the Risen Lord*. Downers Grove, IL: InterVarsity Press, 2010.

Gordon T. Smith, *Evangelical, Sacramental and Pentecostal: Why the Church Should Be All Three*. Downers Grove, IL: InterVarsity Press Academic, 2017.

Gordon T. Smith, *Spiritual Direction: A Guide to Giving and Receiving Direction*. Downers Grove, IL: InterVarsity Press, 2014.

James K.A. Smith, *Desiring the Kingdom: Worship, Worldview, and Cultural Formation*. Grand Rapids, MI: Baker Academic, 2009.

Jean Vanier, *Community and Growth: Our Pilgrimage Together*. Toronto: Griffin, 1979.

Frances Ward, *Lifelong Learning: Theological Education and Supervision*. London: SCM, 2005.

John Webster, *Holy Scripture: A Dogmatic Sketch*. Cambridge: Cambridge University Press, 2003.

Part 3

Fitness

7

Growth: What Difference Does it Make to be a Church Leader?

With this chapter we transition to the second half of the book, which focuses more intently on praxis. By this I mean not to offer silver-bullet prescriptions for ministry, but to shift from the theological framing towards practical ramifications that each leader will have to prayerfully work out within their context and convictions. In the three chapters of Part 3 our focus is on 'fitness': on putting our self-awareness together with contextual awareness for the sake of cooperative participation in church ministry. In the three chapters of Part 4 our focus is on 'decisions'; on the practicalities of planning for missional growth and teamwork in meetings. There are other details one could look at, but the goal of this studyguide is to provide a view of ecclesial praxis from which readers and leaders can launch further. To begin Part 3, we orient ourselves by asking about the goal of church leadership, and how we can tell if we are making a difference. The assumed goal is often 'growth'. But what does that mean?

I used to say I 'grew up' in church. But did I? At what point was I *done* growing? It might be more accurate to say I grew up, am still growing, and hope I always will be growing in and with the church. Growing is not reserved for the children and new people. I find this to be a rather liberating way to think about it, because it frees me from chasing or settling on the illusion of a finalized self, and frees me to trust myself to the growth that God has in store for each season and day of the year. This has been a liberating way to look at my churches too. Churches are never *finished*. This is not to be pictured in the metaphor of high-rise construction zones that are surrounded by cranes and frustratingly never *finished*, but in the biblical metaphors of vines and bodies, which have their basic shape but never quite settle or stay exactly the same. Churches should not be body-shamed towards a photoshopped ideal. They should seek whole-ness and health in the renewal of Word and Spirit. With this perspective we can be less anxious and more secure, without being unadaptable and overconfident. In Christ we can look ourselves over for flowers and fruit, or stretch out our arms to check our reach, without the anxiety of comparing ourselves to some perfect ideal.

But this raises a few questions. For what do we strive if not some measurable goal, some definable project? It is nice to think of ourselves as sunflowers simply stretching up to the sun, but does that really work, psychologically? Where will the drive for growth come from if we are healed of our insecure need to be better, or our competitive drive to be on par with the best? Anxiety and ambi-tion are great motivators. Where will our motivation come from if not from these crutches we have learned to lean on? In some ways there is nothing so anxious as to be cured of anxiety. Is it really so bad to want to *do better*, to *be better*, and to be self-conscious about growth? Is it wrong to want to see fruit, and to be able to say we made a difference? To wrap our minds around this, and to come to grips with what it might mean to be liberated from anxious striving but not from earnest effort, in this chapter we will revisit the perennial question of church growth, asking if there is a good way to look at it. To do so we will revisit the New Testament picture of church growth and read between the lines of its mixed organic metaphors.

Jesus certainly instilled in the apostles a desire to see their fellowship grow to include more people and to take root in more and more places. Their so-called Great Commission was to 'make disciples of all nations' (Matt. 28.18–20), which would require them to bear witness 'to the ends of the earth' in such a way that the works of God might be spoken on every native tongue (Acts 1.6–2.21). As discussed earlier, while the work of the early church did not seem to be organ-ized around numerical increase for its own sake, neither did it take no notice of it (see Acts 2.41–47, 4.32–6.7). Indeed, from the sign of Pentecost to the coun-cil of Jerusalem, the first half of The Acts of the Apostles could justifiably be described as a series of divine promptings to expand their vision towards diverse multiplication beyond their own number and kind (see Acts 2—15). However, in this we should pay careful attention to the fact that the growth of the church proceeded in the mode of faithful responsiveness to God, and never shifted its weight to the front foot of the apostles themselves. When Acts 2 celebrated the first church's increase in numbers, it did not interrupt their devotion to 'teaching and fellowship, to the breaking of bread and the prayers' (2.42). Numerical increase was the footnote, the faithfulness of the disciples was the focus.

The apostles' perspective on growth was entirely in line with the ways they had heard Jesus talk in parables. Consider the following sample:

- Jesus' parable of the seed-sower did celebrate yields of thirty, sixty, and a hundredfold, and did imply that the fruitful would be entrusted with more – but by wildly scattering seed, knowing full well that much of it would not stick, Jesus' sower also defied any inclination to sell our souls to selective efficiency at the expense of open-ended generosity (Matt. 13.1–23).
- Jesus' parable of the shrewd manager appeared at first to defy wastefulness and to approve of the rich master who would lay someone off for it – but by commending the about-to-be-fired manager for using his wealth to gain friends, Jesus illustrated that wealth is not an end in itself: 'You cannot serve God and wealth' (Luke 16.1–13).
- Jesus' parable of the talents accepted that the servant who was 'trustworthy in a few things' could hope to be trusted with more – but the thing that made the servant 'wicked and lazy' was precisely the fact that his scrupulous concern over *the magnitude of the product* hindered his *faithfulness to the job* (Matt. 25.14–31).
- Jesus' parable of the weeds among the wheat celebrated 'when the plants came up and bore grain' – but it also upset agrarian sensibilities in order to counsel against uprooting the weeds before harvest, because only the master himself could separate the wheat from the chaff at the end (Matt. 13.24–30).

Meditation on these parables shows that growth and fruitfulness are worthy aspirations, and that productivity and efficient stewardship are legitimate concerns. But it also shows that faithfulness is not to be sacrificed on the altar of efficiency, nor generosity on the altar of property, nor industry on the altar of projected income, nor patience on the altar of scrupulosity. So Jesus affirms our eagerness to see the church grow in numbers and the kingdom of God branch out on earth, but simultaneously denies our inclination to reorganize church and kingdom to make head-counts and property into ends in themselves.

I mentioned earlier that in my first years of pastoral ministry I had a hard time keeping my head on straight because of the pressure I felt to recalibrate my church according to the means and ends of numerical growth. In the denominational circles in which I travelled, the church growth movement was all the rage, and a good part of it was immensely helpful. As is often the case in a church's life, ours was in need of a season of reflection. Who are we? How are we spending our energies? Do our ministries do what they were originally intended to do? Is our God-talk in language our neighbours would understand? Is our worship expressed in the full range of our voices and experiences? Are our organizational structures helping us or are they needlessly grinding us down? These were good questions, and the *Natural Church Development* (*NCD*) resource we used was geared to help us tackle them. I had some concerns about the way 'church growth' and its measurements were interpreted and communicated, but as an aid to much-needed conversation the *NCD* was very helpful. It got us to gather a representatively diverse group of church people together around the current core of leaders, it gave us exploratory questions we could each answer in discreet confidentiality, and then it arranged our answers in visual clarity so that we could have a candid and constructive conversation. What I found most helpful was the fact that the *NCD* resource insisted that our job as a church was not to manufacture growth, but to aim for health and let God do the growing. What I found least helpful about it was that the measure of our church's *health* was still ultimately couched in terms of its numerical growth. For all the good that was there, this underlying premise was still liable to do some damage.

Drawing from the New Testament's organic metaphors for the church, *NCD* pointed out that just as gardeners do not actually *grow* plants, but patiently and attentively tend to their *health*, so too it is not ours to *grow* churches, but to *tend to their health*. Growth is God's problem. Our task is to be faithful. Growth can be desired and celebrated, but it is not a reliable metric to work around, and so should not sidetrack us from simple obedience. Sometimes faithfulness can mean persisting through a time of decrease, taking the time to re-evaluate without wringing our hands in fear. Faithfulness can even mean closing a church's doors or merging it with another, if that is how God so leads. This can be done with lamentation, but that is not the same thing as saying it is done in shame. What would be a shame would be to strive in a direction God is *not* leading, simply because of our presumption that the show must go on, that bigger is better, and that all that matters is more.

We can see these nuances in Jesus' parables, but how do they play out in the letters of the New Testament, those biblical snapshots of the apostles' efforts to work this out in the early church? Taking the letter to the Ephesians as a representative sample, the focus on health over growth rings true. As a matter of fact, the way Ephesians talks about growth has much more to do with the hopes of maturity than the metrics of a market. What difference does it make to be a church leader? In Ephesians we learn that it got Paul put in prison! And from prison he put it to the church with piercing clarity, exhorting them to 'lead a life worthy of the calling' that is given to 'each of us' as 'grace according to the measure of Christ's gift' (4.1–7). Then, after the reminder that Jesus ascended precisely so that he might send back these gifts (8–11), Paul spells out what is the difference church leadership hopes to make:

> Equip the saints for the work of ministry, for building up the body of Christ, until all of us come to the unity of the faith and of the knowledge of the Son of God, to maturity, to the measure of the full stature of Christ. (4.12–13)

We will come back to what it says we are supposed to do about this in a moment, but first we fast forward two verses to ensure we get the point. The charge continues:

> Grow up in every way into him who is the head, into Christ, from whom the whole body, joined and knitted together by every ligament with which it is equipped, as each part is working properly, promotes the body's growth in building itself up in love. (4.15–16)

The difference church leaders seek is maturity, both as it applies to the formation of a gift-sharing community and as it applies to its grace-sharing members.

There is a dynamic interrelationship between the maturity of the group and the maturity of its various members, and what the leader hopes for most of all is to tend to the health of that social ecology, promoting health and growth in Christ. What this requires is spelled out in the verses between:

> We must no longer be children, tossed to and fro and blown about by every wind of doctrine, by people's trickery, by their craftiness in deceitful scheming. But speaking the truth in love, we must grow up in every way into him who is the head, into Christ. (4.14–15)

In light of this passage it appears unfortunate if we think of 'spiritual formation' in terms of individual 'Christ-likeness' alone, rather than participation in the formation of Christ's body on earth. To flourish as a Christian individual is to find one's place in a healthy church. To mature as a member of a maturing church is far better for an individual than to see church merely as a service station on the road to what is ultimately an individualized destination. The Christian life is not a self-help guide to self-fulfilment any more than the church is a communitarian project that proceeds at the expense of its members. If we set these things against each other we end up giving up one or the other. Neither is an end in itself; both have their end in God, and are held together in real time in the presence and work of the reconciling Christ, and in the power and the fellowship of the Holy Spirit. When the church is healthy it is experienced as neither a competitive market nor an inhumane corporation. Where two or three are gathered in Jesus name for reconciliation, there Christ is on earth, working towards the flourishing of both the individual and the community.

Numerical growth can be destructive if it is spreading discord or erasing diversity. Put starkly, the question is whether we are a spiralling vine or a destructive tornado, whether we are intertwining like branches or curving in on ourselves like ingrown toenails. The difference is whether we are tossed around by crafty schemes or are growing in truth and love. The difference is a matter of maturity – which is not to say it is a matter of age. If it is true that grey hair can be a sign of wisdom, so too can youth be wise beyond their years. Experience and education are no guarantee of maturity. A senior citizen can be more wily and wicked than a teenager, and a long-time church-member can be more toxic than a newcomer. In Ephesians the reference to children and grown ups is not an evaluative grid but an illustration. The truth is that children can be mature, just as grown-ups can be immature. The point is to ask where maturity can be found. The answer is that it is found in being 'joined and knitted' to Christ. A Christian does not join others simply as a means to the end of self-development. Nor does a church engulf individuals merely as a means to a strategic end. The two go hand-in-hand as they are reconciled in the work of Christ.

We see this in Jesus' commandment to 'love your neighbour as yourself' (Matt. 22.39). Some conclude that before you can love your neighbours you have to learn to love yourself, but this is not what Jesus said. The way Jesus put it certainly implied that so-called self-love will be intertwined with love of others, but the order matters. If we only ever love others to the degree that we love ourselves, not only will we succumb to the never-ending vortex of self-care, but we will also find ways to love others in a self-serving way. This is the great danger of the so-called 'golden rule' when it is pulled out of its context in the law and the prophets (see Matt. 7.12): we do unto others what we want done to ourselves, and carry on assuming that we know best. Unchecked by God we carry on in the sin of self-centred self-direction, even and especially in what looks like love for others. We make an idol out of self-giving, at the expense of other-receiving, and manage to turn even the best of things into the worst. Such is the corruption of sin in the human heart, not to mention the systems of humankind. But if we take the lead of the one who fulfilled the law and the prophets and informed the golden rule, we come back to the Great Commandment and find that love of neighbour and wholeness of self – heart, mind, soul, and body – is found entirely in love of God.

No wonder even 'self control' is named by the apostle Paul as a fruit *of the Spirit*. Against self control there may be no law, but it grows as we 'live by the Spirit' (Gal. 5.22–25). The alternative is to 'become conceited, competing against one another' with envy (5.26) – and 'those who do such things will not inherit the kingdom of God' (21). The modern obsession with self-fulfilment, self-direction, self-control, and self-security distorts everything, both for individuals and for groups. Theologically speaking, self-security is the epitome of insecurity.

To borrow a word from Edwin Friedman's *A Failure of Nerve: Leadership in the Age of the Quick Fix*, we might say that the important thing is not love of self, but a self that is properly 'differentiated' (p. 194). However, where Friedman places the emphasis is on the *self's* ability to differentiate from other selves, we would point to the commands of Christ and say that the self that is given wholly to God is thus given to others as a differentiated self. This contrasts the logics of independence-driven competition or acceptance-driven co-dependency. A degree of independence is good, but total independence is an illusion, and full autonomy is simply not good. A degree of dependence on others is thus also good, but total dependence on others (i.e. co-dependency) is generally not a sign of personal or relational health. If we are co-dependent it is usually either temporary (in a time of healing or growth) or is relative to age or impairment. Even in these cases, however, a good caregiver will promote as much independence as possible in order to be a respecter of the person and an encourager of personal identity and growth. While each has its place, neither dependence nor independence is the human goal. Those who wave the magic wand of 'balance' at this tension merely settle for an abstraction. The question remains who or what will manage the balancing act: the autonomous, self-directed individual, or the all-encompassing group? Then the question is who or what will balance *that*?

Edwin Friedman and others provide helpful theories about family systems and differentiated persons, many of which can be recommended for adaptation, but the Christian endeavour to wrestle with these tensions still needs to begin and end with God. Dietrich Bonhoeffer's *Discipleship* explains this poignantly:

> It is true, there is something which comes between persons called by Christ and the given circumstances of their natural lives. But it is not someone unhappily contemptuous of life; it is not some law of piety. Instead it is life and the gospel itself; it is Christ himself. In becoming human, he put himself between me and the given circumstances of the world. I cannot go back. He is in the middle … *He is the mediator*, not only between God and human persons, but also between person and person, and between person and reality … Even the way to the 'God-given reality' of that other person, with whom I live, must go through Christ, or it is a wrong way. (pp. 93–6)

It is Christ who gives us our individuality – 'for to me, living is Christ, dying is gain' (Phil. 1.21) – and it is in the grace of Christ and the love of God that we have 'the communion of the Holy Spirit' (2 Cor. 13.13). As Bonhoeffer continues:

> According to the will of Jesus, we are called one way or another out of imme-diate relationships, and we must become single individuals, visibly or secretly. But it is precisely this same mediator who makes us into individuals, who be-comes the basis for entirely *new community*. He stands in the center between the other person and me. He separates, but also unites. (p. 98)

The message of the Bible and the ministry of the church is interdependence in the family of God, wherein each of our identities is differentiated and worked out over time in the love of God by the mediation of Christ, and interwoven in the guidance and the fellowship of the Spirit.

The problem with the question *what difference does a church leader make*, then, is that it can play into the idea that the leader has got to be everything, rather than play their God-given part, leaving it to God to make the difference. This means that God makes the difference in terms of results, but also does the 'differentiating' between individual parts, not rigidly according to the social roles and norms of empire or economics, or of family dynamics or church politics, but in real time as the Spirit apportions grace to each and all. In other words, those whose security is in God's love for them, whose worth is in serving the Lord, and whose services are as given by the Spirit, will be the ones who make a difference for maturity rather than for immaturity. This is the case no matter what our age or education or experience.

Unfortunately we are insecure, broken people. This is the condition that our sin has plunged us into, and it is freedom from this for which we long. Denying it does not do us any good, but dying to self and rising in Christ will do. In this way it is not far from the truth when people say that church leaders should 'lead from their brokenness', if by that we mean humble and repentant, authentic and open about the laying of one's sins and successes at the feet of the Lord. However, we should not twist this into the idea that we lead from our insecurity. That way on its own leads to the combativeness of undifferentiated selves observed by Friedman, the social effect of which others have described in terms of toxic triangulations. When everybody is consciously or unconsciously angling to feel better about themselves, the easiest way is to get one up on the people around. So instead of speaking truth in love to one another in the security of our Christ-confession, we 'triangulate' every situation to try to stay on top, to try to steer clear of the fray, to passive aggressively get our way. It is not usually maliciously intended; we just cannot help it. Unchecked by the love of God and unrenewed in God's grace each day, we are liable to continue to live and lead from insecurity alone, thus sowing the seeds of insecurity and immaturity in others. We think the antidote to insecurity is self-security when it is wholeness in Christ and the freeing of the Spirit for differentiated fellowship.

I have battled with insecurity my whole life. This has been easy for people to guess when it has manifested itself as shyness or self-deprecation, but those are not always accurate perceptions. Sometimes good things get misinterpreted under the unfortunate banner of shyness, and self-deprecation gets misperceived as self-pity. But those are not the worst of the misperceptions, since insecurity is often most brazen just when a person appears most confident and assertive. Speaking for myself, there are times when I know I have come across very confidently, but the truth has been anything but. What appears confident can feel like an embarrassingly transparent attempt to clamour and cover up some point of weakness. Appearances can be deceptive. This would be one thing on its own, but what I am interested in here is the social dynamics of insecurity wherein a social group can become a breeding ground for competitive self-assertion, or destructive self-loathing, all under the guise of humility. The results can be toxic, and if they are not careful leaders will play into this brokenness rather than lead out of it.

When I was starting out in ministry I was headed for trouble in this regard. The way I used to deal with my lack of social confidence was to remember the adage people told me about neighbourhood dogs, which was that they are more afraid of me than I am of them. As a mental trick it has been helpful from time to time, but even when it rings true it is not a lasting comfort. When I think back to what helped me start to deal with my insecurity, I am reminded of a college leadership retreat led by Tim Elmore in which he named it as a common problem and a call to trust God. What stuck with me was when he named a number of 'symptoms of insecurity' we could identify and hand over to Christ, not only for the sake of personal growth in sanctification but relational interdependence in the fellowship of the Holy Spirit. My notes from that day are hardly publishable, but Elmore has since posted similar reflections on the *Growing Leaders* website in an exhortation towards 'emotional intelligence'. There he lists five 'weapons of a leader's self-destruction' which leaders need to guard against:

1 Projecting their self-worth.
2 Clinging to a scarcity perspective.
3 Possessing a controlling spirit.
4 Comparing themselves to others obsessively.
5 Possessing self-imposed blindness.

In this list I think we can readily see the pitfalls of leadership that plague us due to our human disconnect from God and one another in the fragmentation of original sin. It exposes some of the ways we cope with our brokenness, often perpetuating the damage to self and others, even if it is only in long-term intangible ways. We do this by: (1) compensating to cover up our weaknesses; (2) outperforming to cover for what we presume to be a scarcity of allies; (3) asserting (or hiding) our wishes to cover from the threat of others; (4) overstating (or under-stating) our worth to cover any comparison to others; and/or (5) over-writing our life-narratives to cover over uncomfortable incidents or insights and keep them within self-imposed limits. There are numerous other psychological and sociological pathologies which could be named. The point is not to wallow in these and further our sense of woe, but to turn these things over to God in prayer, give them to Christ, and receive new life from the Spirit. As such these personal and relational diagnostics can serve as tools for confessional prayer, just as long as they do not take on a life of their own and usurp the mediation of Christ. I suspect the pathologies of insecurity have managed to worm their way into more lives than just mine, and more churches than just those I have observed. But this is not meant to be a downer. What I think these reflections help us recognize is that our drive for observable growth and measurable difference can so easily be a reflection of our pathological drive to compare and compete, rather than a healthy aspect of our pursuit of the gifts and the fruit of the Spirit. We all need to be freed to live and lead in the security of the love of God. What we seek is growth in maturity, both as individuals who find their identity in Christ's mediation of the Creator's grace to them, and as churches who find themselves intertwined in the upbuilding fellowship of the Spirit. To confess this is need can be the first step of freedom to lead in Jesus' name.

It is not wrong to want to make a difference. It is not unhealthy to want to see fruit. But it is important that we look at moments of measurable growth as milestones to be celebrated rather than standards to be set in themselves. It is perfectly legitimate for churches to commit to projects and to work them out faithfully together, but this is a far cry from setting targets and realigning everything to manage effectiveness to the extension of our self-wrought plans and schemes. If growth in numbers is a goal we cannot manipulate or measure ourselves by, and health is the goal we are to attend to faithfully, then the question *what difference a leader makes* has more to do with maturity than with metrics of increase. Milestones of church health and missional multiplication may still be celebrated or lamented along the way, we realize that the difference a leader makes cannot be dislocated from the valleys and hills of mundane life together. The mature leader seeks neither to stand out or to shrink away, but looks for their God-given place in the body of Christ, and as such in their neighbourhood, country, and world. There are no shortcuts to this. It might be retroactively traced out and seen for its mountains and valleys, but in the meantime it is pursued along the lines of the Great Commission and Commandments in the grace of Christ each day. Thus what Friedman calls a 'differentiated' leader we would call a person who is daily renewed in the love of God to the reconciliation of heart, soul, mind, and body in Christ, not for the end-game of self-fulfilment but of Christ's reconciling work among neighbours and strangers, enemies and friends, leading out of his death and resurrection and reign. A key part of that work is the gathering of local bodies of Christ-confessing community who thus witness to the Spirit's work of new creation. To be a church leader is humbling but happy work.

So when it comes to church growth, a maturing Body of Christ is the goal. This frames the particular goals and practices of church leadership quite uniquely. A mature Christian leader *contributes* to a church's health and growth, rather than achieving it like a superhero. In the next chapter, then, we will discuss what this means with regard to the discernment of spiritual gifts and callings.

Further reflection

Reflect on the symptoms of 'self-destructive leaders' listed by Tim Elmore and focus on one or two which might manifest themselves in your own life. Confess any deeply ingrained personal baggage, habits, or sins from which you need freedom.

Use the Great Commandment as a kind of diagnostic for confessional prayer, identifying specifics to ask Christ to grow in the love of God. For the sake of the exercise, let each part represent the following aspects of life:

Heart – emotion and desire.
Soul – will and ambition.
Mind – attention and understanding.
Body – physicality and place.
Neighbour – friends and strangers.

Read one of the parables referred to in this chapter and compile pros and cons regarding the methodical pursuit of numerical growth in the church. Name the warnings and the wisdom for the stewarding of church resources and 'reach'.

Further reading

Dietrich Bonhoeffer, *Dietrich Bonhoeffer Works 4: Discipleship*, trans. B. Green
and R. Krauss, ed. G.B. Kelly and J.D. Godsey. Minneapolis, MN: Fortress,
2001 [1937].
Tim Elmore, 'Self-Destructive Leaders,' on the *Growing Leaders* website (as of
July 2018), at https://growingleaders.com/blog/self-destructive-leaders.
Edwin H. Friedman, *A Failure of Nerve: Leadership in the Age of the Quick Fix*,
ed. M.M. Treadwell and E.W. Beal. New York: Seabury Books, 1999.
David Hoyle, *The Pattern of our Calling: Ministry Yesterday, Today and Tomorrow*.
London: SCM Press, 2016.

8

Charisma: What Does it Take to Run a Church?

My teenage self would have been appalled and terrified to learn that my early twenties would see me training for pastoral ministry. Not only did I not want this in my life, but by personality and aptitude I felt ill-suited for it in every way. But church leadership is not necessarily a product of our natural skills or proclivities; it is a calling and a gift that comes from God, an interruption of grace into otherwise-directed lives. Sometimes we get tapped on the shoulder to lead because of a proximate match between the position and our personalities, experiences, and skills of course, and this can be entirely appropriate. It can even be the *way* we come to discover a gift and a call to church leadership. After all, it is not as if the spiritual call is necessarily *opposed* to our natural abilities. But neither are the two equated. But if we cannot *rely* on indicators of aptitude, experience, personality, and education, how do we tell if we have what it takes?

The New Testament suggests that leadership is a spiritual gift, and that the roles we take up in the church are to be discerned and maintained primarily as callings from God. But what this does this mean and how is it discerned? Could one accept a leadership role *without* the spiritual gift of leadership? If leadership is a spiritual gift, who has it? Who needs it? How does it function with the other gifts of God's grace to the church? These questions are worth exploring because the way we answer them will have an impact not only on the maturing of our self-awareness, but also on the shape of our approach to leadership (and other ministries) in the church. In the next two chapters we will explore the biblical teaching on spiritual gifts in the hope that this will put us on the right track and help us to find our place and get a feel for the unique way the Spirit might be wiring us to operate within it.

We have already looked at Ephesians 4 and seen how vital it is to the unity and integrity of the church that 'each of us [is] given grace according to the measure of Christ's gift', and that these are given 'for building up the body of Christ' (4.7–12). These verses explicitly name the apostle, prophet, evangelist, pastor, and teacher as roles for which some in the church will be gifted and set apart (11–12). For reasons that will become clear, we will return to these in Chapter 9. But the letters of the New Testament return to this topic several times. In this chapter we will first draw from Romans 12.1–8, 1 Corinthians 12—14, Ephesians 4.1–16 and 1 Peter 4.7–11 in order to give definition to what 'spiritual gifts' are about and to gather an inventory of those that are named. We will then reflect on 1 Corinthians to draw out key insights about how these gifts work for the good of the church.

In Romans 12 and Ephesians 4 the word-pairing of 'grace' [*charis*] and 'give' [*didomi*] comes to epitomize the functional inner life of the church, showing it to be a people bound together in mutual service to the living God.

> By the *grace given* me I say … we have gifts that differ according to the *grace given* to us. (Rom. 12.3,6)

> Each of us was *given grace* according to the measure of Christ's gift. (Eph. 4.7)

In 1 Peter 4 and 1 Corinthians 12—14 these notions are held together with the words for 'receive' [*lambano*] and 'spiritual' things [*pneumatikos*], adding up to an unmistakable cumulative effect.

> Like good stewards of the manifold *grace* of God, serve one another with whatever *gift* each of you has *received*. (1 Pet. 4.10)

> Now concerning *spiritual* gifts, brothers and sisters, I do not want you to be uninformed … Now there are varieties of *gifts*, but the same Spirit; and there are varieties of services, but the same Lord; and there are varieties of activities, but it is the same God who activates all of them in everyone. To each is *given* the manifestation of the Spirit for the common good. (1 Cor. 12.1,4–7)

Put together, these passages teach that the church is a unified but diverse communion in Christ. This unity is not found in uniformity but diversity, and the nature of that diversity is not just seen in its cultures and personalities (although there is variety there too), but is primarily upheld in the diverse services we provide to one another. After its profound teaching about the boundary-crossing politics of the Lord's Supper, 1 Corinthians begins chapter 12 by ensuring readers do not miss how the church is supposed to work: What makes the difference between the religion of mute idols and the spirituality of the church is that the Spirit leads us to speak and share the words and gifts of the living Lord Jesus Christ (12.1–3).

To use the language of the passages above, then, the life of the church is one where diverse graces – or spiritual gifts – are given and received, all worked out in and through us by one and the same Triune God. Based on the word for a spiritual gift, χάρισμα (*charisma*), this is what we call the charismatic nature of the church. Because this word can have a number of meanings in modern English, it is vital that we ensure we are using it the way it is meant with respect to leadership in the church.

In modern society the word 'charismatic' has been popularized to refer to someone who is able to get people to *want* to follow them, either by force of enthusiasm or eloquence or some other form of social sway. For almost a century, the label *charismatic* has been a common way of distinguishing influential modes of leadership from *hierarchical* or *bureaucratic* modes, thanks to the work of sociologist Max Weber (1864–1920). For Weber, if authority was traditionally dispersed according to accepted *hierarchies*, and *bureaucracy* was a way of re-dispersing it according to the roles opened up by agreed governing structures (Weber, p. 328), then *charismatic* authority names 'a certain quality of an individual personality by virtue of which he [or she] is set apart from ordinary' people as one with 'exceptional qualities' and thus worth following (p. 358). Weber was tracing the same shift from ancient-authoritarian to modern-individualist leadership that we unpacked in Chapter 1 with respect to Alasdair MacIntyre's depictions of the Rich Aesthete, the Manager, and the Therapist. In a sense MacIntyre was simply naming the three modern types of *charisma* which make the difference between a leader we will *tolerate* and a leader we will *follow* – no matter what our formal governing structures happen to be. It rings true that a 'charismatic leader' tends to be a persuasive communicator, a dynamic mobilizer of effectiveness, or a contagious purveyor of warmth, charm, or perspective.

In church circles the popular use of 'charismatic' comes closer to its biblical meaning, but has tended to refer primarily to a narrow slice of the spiritual gifts that are named in Scripture, largely due to the momentum of two movements that swept Christianity in the past two centuries: the Pentecostal and Charismatic movements. Although a vital emphasis in these movements has been the full participation of each believer in the ministries of the Holy Spirit, the fact that this has been most dramatically manifested in ecstatic speech (i.e. 'tongues') and 'gifts [*charismata*] of healing' (1 Cor. 12.9–11) has led us to narrow the meaning of 'charismatic' to refer to these more spectacular gifts. Combined with the popular understanding of a dynamic leader mentioned above, this has unfortunately made 'charismatic' mean almost the opposite of what it means in the letters of the New Testament. If the apostles of the early church were using the word 'charisma' to point away from the fixation on powerful and persuasive leadership to the diversified functioning of ministry-sharing believers, then there's a tragic irony if modern use of the same word now supports a focus on dynamic or spectacular leaders at the expense of the mundane services of mutual discipleship. I say this not to downplay the significance of the Charismatic movement or to denounce the more dramatic gifts, but to suggest that the real promise of the movement is in its fullest flourishing, not in its narrowing.

We will return to the place of such gifts in a moment, but first we need to restate the important point that *charismatic* is not just a buzzword for one flavour of Christianity, but is something that all churches are by definition meant to be. A Roman Catholic congregation could operate more charismatically than a Pentecostal one, if that means it has a vibrant life of spiritual gift sharing. But we need not pit the streams of Christianity against each other; the point is to emphasize this common dynamic they ought to share. Where the Charismatic movement has prompted renewal in this regard it has been a gift to the ecumenical Church. No matter which denomination and organizational structure we find ourselves in, this has profound implications for church leadership, which we will discuss further in Chapter 9. First, however, we need to understand what the spiritual gifts are and how they work together. So in the rest of this chapter we will gather a list of the kinds of spiritual gifts named in the biblical passages above, and then put them in practical-theological perspective with help from 1 Corinthians 12—14.

The activities named in Romans 12, 1 Corinthians 12—14, Ephesians 4, and 1 Peter 4 do not appear to be intended as a scientific organizational chart, providing distinct containers into which we can vacuum-seal ourselves. When they are gathered together in a list they do seem extensive enough to be considered fairly comprehensive, but it could be that there are ministries that do not fit neatly into them. In that event, however, it can still be fruitful to find a biblically named spiritual gift to which a contemporary ministry bears a family resemblance, and to reconcile ourselves to the historical guidance of Word and Spirit. There are numerous resources which compile spiritual gift 'inventories' and provide questionnaires to match up to them like personality styles, but we will not tread that same ground here. Instead we will name and briefly define them, and recommend asking your church for a preferred questionnaire if such a thing is desirable. Such an activity can be helpful as long as the results are seen as talking points for conversation with trusted others rather than as definitive categories into which you are pigeon-holed for the rest of time.

While the spiritual gifts are not strictly scientific, it can be illuminating to picture them like the periodic table of elements. This makes a better analogy than a personality test because the latter tends to paint us into a corner whereas the former helps us think of the spiritual gifts as component parts that work together in unique and fluid combinations to give us life as we know it. In everyday life we do not typically encounter the elements of the periodic table in the isolated purity of petri dishes but in the chemical combinations that make up the gases, liquids and solids by which we live. Even a pure iron chair only really achieves the fullness of its iron chair-ness when it is supports the weight of that which it was meant to carry, which will tend to be an oxygen-breathing person made up of mostly carbon and water. So too we might sometimes encounter people who seem to perfectly fit the mould of one gift or another, but even then this will not be experienced in its fullness without collaboration with the other gift-giving members of the church. Nor should we expect it to be fixed that way for all time. That does not mean there is no value in identifying gifts that the Spirit appears to be giving to you and through you, but it relativizes this exercise considerably.

So to help us get our bearings as church leaders, let us look at the different spiritual gifts or *charisms* named by each of our four passages, and take brief note of the activities they might entail. We will work our way around the periodic table of spiritual gifts provided (see Table 2) in order to get a sense of possible family resemblances between gifts and of the notional proximity they have to one another in church experience. Again, this is not to pin the charisms down like a dead butterfly collection, but to get a sense of the chemical reactions that take place in the body of Christ as the Spirit brings it together through the enlivening of its working parts.

Table 2: Periodic chart of spiritual gifts

Eph. 4.11 **A** 1 Cor. 12.28–29					Eph. 4.11 **P** Rom. 12.6 1 Cor. 12.10, 28–29
Hy 1 Pet. 4.9	**Gi** Rom. 12.8	**Me** Rom. 12.8	1 Cor. 12.28 **Hs** Rom. 12.7	**Ex** Rom. 12.8	**Wi** 1 Cor. 12.8
Fa 1 Cor. 12.9	**Mi** 1 Cor. 12.10, 28–29	**Hg** 1 Cor. 12.9, 28, 30	Eph. 4.11 **S**	**Di** 1 Cor. 12.10	**Kn** 1 Cor. 12.8
Eph. 4.11 **E**	**To** 1 Cor. 12.10; 14.22 Acts 2.1–11	**In** 1 Cor. 12.10; 14.13	**Ad** 1 Cor. 12.28	**Lp** Rom. 12.8	Eph. 4.11 **T** Rom. 12.7 1 Cor. 12.28–29

Apostleship

When Christ ascended he sent delegates or messengers (*apostolous*) to equip the saints to build up his church (Eph. 4.11). In Acts they are church planters and theologians. They included the seemingly gregarious Paul and Peter, but apostleship is not reducible to a spiritual ideal or a personality style. Not everyone is meant to be an apostle (1 Cor. 12.28–29), and apostles can be as varied as Barnabas, Thomas and Junia. We will return to this (along with the next four gifts) in Chapter 9.

Prophecy

When Christ fulfilled the prophets (Matt. 5.17) he fully revealed the divine Word so that everyone thereafter might prophesy or profess the wonder of God (Acts 2.5–21). Like apostleship, however, the particular gift of prophecy (*propheteia*) is not *expected* of everyone all the time (1 Cor. 12.10, 28–29; Eph. 4.11), even if all are *encouraged* to be eager for it in their pursuit of love (1 Cor. 14.1). As a gift it entails the expounding of God's Word 'in proportion to faith' (Rom. 12.6) as it relates to the circumstances of the faith-community, as seen in Peter's sermon and in the regular ministries of Apollos, Priscilla and Aquila (Acts 18).

Evangelism

When Christ's good news (*euangelia*) is shared it can involve first time exposures to the gospel or to the perennial task of bringing it into focus for believers (2 Tim. 4.1–5). Those who are called to the particular ministry of evangelism (*euangelistas*) will both introduce and reintroduce us to the gospel (Eph. 4.11–15).

Shepherding

When Christ the shepherd showed himself willing to leave the fold to chase down one stray, he also charged the flock with the same ministry of merciful, moral and relational reconciliation (Matt. 18.10–20). Within this universal calling, some are set apart specifically as shepherds (*poimenas*) for the oversight and exercise of the church's ministry of pastoral care (Eph. 4.11).

Teaching

When Christ spent years revealing to the disciples that he was the very Word of God in flesh, he was also preparing them to see him in the Scriptures and to extend the ministry of prayerful study and instruction by which he would continue to make himself known (Luke 24). Not all are teachers (*didaskalous*), but all are to be taught (1 Cor. 12.28–29; Eph. 4.11; Rom. 12.7).

Leadership

The above gifts all seem likely to involve leading, but a distinct gift of leadership (*proistamenos*) or presidency is also named among them, which is to be done with due diligence (Rom. 12.8). Linked to the office of elder (*presbyterous*), this gift might be closest to shepherding and teaching, as it suggests oversight and direction of the gathered life and ministries of the church (1 Tim. 5.17). The charge to diligence licenses a degree of intentionality and efficiency, just as long as these serve rather than usurp the church's purposes.

Administration

The gift of administration (*kubernesis*) is also sometimes translated leadership, but might be closer to navigation than presidency, like piloting a ship according to determined coordinates (1 Cor. 12.28). Administrators are those gifted and authorized to organize people and tasks, coordinating and enabling them in keeping with the church's mission. If not overseers (*episkopes*), they might be deacons (*diakanoi*) like Phoebe, who was to be well-received and provided with what she needed to help others (Rom. 16.1–2; 1 Tim. 3.1–13).

Helps

The gift of helps gathers up what appear to be the very similar ministries of assistance (*antilepsis*, 1 Cor. 12.28) and service (*diakonian*, Rom. 12.7). The latter puts it briskly: if your gift is service, serve. To this 1 Peter 4.11 adds that 'whoever serves must do so with the strength that God supplies, so that God may be glorified in all things through Jesus Christ'. These directions are profound in their simplicity, addressing those who for all their willing service *to God* can also get roped in to doing otherwise.

Discernment

Among the spiritual gifts is discernment (*diakriseis*) of the spirits (1 Cor. 12.10). It may be that some are inclined to intuit other's motives or spiritual bearings, but this is not clearly referenced in the text, and we should be cautious about reducing this gift to a 'sense'. Hebrews 5.13–14 suggests the immature user of this gift will be 'unskilled in the word of righteousness', whereas 'the mature' will be 'those whose faculties have been trained by practice to distinguish good from evil'. However intuitive this gift might be, it grows in the well-studied practice of moral and ministerial discernment. One situation in which it might flourish is when people are looking to come to grips with their callings in life and ministry.

Knowledge

The gift of 'the utterance of knowledge' (*gnoseos*) seems to identify a God-given aptitude for preparing and providing informed insight on various matters (1 Cor. 12.8). There may be initial hunches involved in the exercise of this gift, but Colossians 2.2–4 warns against deception by 'plausible arguments,' instead exhorting the 'riches of assured understanding' in 'the knowledge of God's mystery, that is, Christ himself, in whom are hidden all the treasures of wisdom and knowledge'.

Wisdom

The word of wisdom (*logos sophias*) works with the word of knowledge (1 Cor. 12.28) by submitting gathered human intelligence to the divine revelation of our finite, fallen situation, and understanding from this how to live. 1 Corinthians suggests that the natural and social sciences are *reconcilable* with divine wisdom, but without the fear of the Lord will stumble over a crucified Christ, whose 'weakness is stronger than human strength' (1 Cor. 1.25). One can see how this gift might come close to the prophetic, since it may not infrequently put us in the position of speaking truth to power and advocating for the vulnerable.

Exhortation

Those whose gift is exhortation (*parakaleo*) are called to prompt others to pursue what God has for them (Rom. 12.8). If there is a distinction between this and the gifts named above it may be in the nuance of Paul's letters to Timothy, where exhortation is closely aligned to the pastoral work of teaching (1 Tim. 4.13) and involves convincing and rebuking with timely words or inconvenient truths, 'with the utmost patience' (2 Tim. 4.2).

Faith

Faith is a given in all Christian life and ministry, but the distinct gift of faith (*pistis*) is the Spirit's provision to address a particular situation (1 Cor. 12.9). It seems that this fruit of the Spirit is experienced as a particular gift to the church through those who 'keep the faith' for others, as it were. In James 5.13–20 we see faith operative for others in circumstances of sickness, downheartedness, sin, and straying from truth, and it appears to be manifested most explicitly in the pattern of intercessory prayer. Faith is rather abstract until it is put to work in faithfulness (James 2.14–26). It is not exactly something that can be recreated and verified empirically – it is always a fruit of the Spirit (Gal. 5.22). Faith connects with God's larger project. Those 'commended for their faith' in Hebrews 11 'did not receive what was promised, since God had provided something better so that they would not, apart from us, be made perfect' (11.39–40).

Tongues

When first experienced in the early church, the sign of tongues was a divinely bestowed ability to speak in a language unknown to the speaker, which set a trajectory for the gospel to be known in every dialect of earth (Acts 1.8—2.14). When the gift of tongues (*glosson*) was exercised in the church at Corinth it remained akin to that initial missionary sign of Pentecost (1 Cor. 12.10,28,30), but was experienced in a prayer language that was more intimate than rational (14.1–16). Unlike the surrounding gnostic mystery cults, however, the Corinthians were not to let this become an insider's secret, since those spiritually gifted *in Christ* are not to be self-serving but other-focused in love (13.1–13). In the church context, then, while they are not strictly forbidden, tongues always seek and defer to interpretation, aiming to be hospitably communicable and peaceably intelligible (14.16–40). Interestingly, tongues without interpretation is closer to evangelism, since it is 'a sign not for believers but for unbelievers' (14.22), who will either dismiss it or join in the shared pursuit of the God made known in Christ (14.22–25). Like those among whom seed was scattered in Jesus' parable of the sower, they will either hear and fall away, or hear and then come to understand (Matt. 9.1–23). Just like at Pentecost, then, tongues stoke the fire of mission, since it is the gift of the Spirit moving us forward into yet unknown languages, which we rely on others to help us understand.

Interpretation

The person who can make sense of what a tongues-speaker is saying is to exercise the gift of interpretation (*hermeneia*), thus bringing the embers of faith to full flame in the other-reaching love of Christian community (1 Cor. 12.10, 30). Unique among the gifts for its explicit co-dependence with another, this pairing of interpretation with tongues serves as a reminder of the eccentricity of the faith (by which I mean both its uniqueness and its trajectory towards others). Apart from the content of what is said, then, the interpreter offers an act of cultural–linguistic connection which not only conveys but models the good news of reconciliation. This gift bridges the evangelistic and the pastoral, and if it includes the hard work of translation may also be akin to administration and teaching.

Miracles

Mentioned alongside healing, the gift of miracles (*dunameis*) is by definition the most unusual of them all (1 Cor. 12.10,28–29). This gift is best understood in the light of the ministry of Jesus and the apostles, who performed signs and wonders not as ends in themselves but as a testament of the Creator's power and love. It is not clear whether there were many (if any) miracles which did not serve someone's tangible need for freedom from suffering or oppression. A person with the gift of miracles may expose gaps in health care and natural resource sharing – not to undermine the exercise of those socio-economic systems, but to prompt and support them towards justice and peace. Whether miracles are spectacular exceptions to the rule or momentary unveilings of the Spirit's abiding work in the mundane, they remind us that the gifts of God are not entitlements but remain reliant upon the Spirit.

Healing

The gifts of healing (*iamaton*) are not outlined in detail, but clearly involve addressing those who are suffering and praying that they may be made well (1 Cor. 12.9,28,30). The giver of this gift will be prompted by the Spirit to ask if a person is suffering and in need of prayer, and though they might look for healing there and then, will be prepared to stick it out with the person as a bridge to the church's solidarity, offering to 'call for the elders of the church and have them pray over them, anointing them with oil in the name of the Lord' (James 5.13–16). Just as miracles prompt mundane justice, as tongues look for interpretation, and as faith works itself out in love, so there is no reason to assume that healing takes place *at the expense of* health care. Indeed, the prophets and apostles exhort the church to extend their concern beyond the confines of the believing community, such that the gift of healing is as likely to be seen in patient social work as in the spontaneous recoveries of believers. There is no need for an either/or between the spiritual and the medical. Those with this gift ought to be prayerful and careful, attending to the whole person rather than reducing everything to the immediacy of physical impairment. Sensitive to emotional and relational concerns, those with gifts of healing are likely to rub up against systems that disable and oppress. They seek to be artful and informed in the way they promote social justice by coming alongside to encourage people's flourishing and inclusion.

Mercy

The gift of mercy is similar to those above in that it refers to something that is basic to all Christians but is also exhibited in particular ways by some as a gift to the rest. When the gift of mercy (*eleon*) is listed in Romans 12.8 it is something *enacted cheerfully* or *readily*. This implies a contrast to philanthropic pity, altruistic lenience, or guilt-riddled aid. The giver of mercy may *develop* a high degree of empathy but mercy does not *need* to feel sympathy or to see something deserving in the other before it is given. This gift entails a readiness to act on behalf of others for no other reason than that they lack something God has meant for all to share. This could be manifest in direct acts of compassion or indirect spurs to community action. Those with the gift of mercy are not above others looking down at them, but are enraptured by a vision of the Creator's full and unhindered shalom reaching every nook and cranny of creation.

Giving

Giving is essential to all the gifts, but there is a particular gift of giving (*metadidous*) which appears to involve the supply of tangible needs over and above what we might give dutifully or begrudgingly as citizens – it is an expression of the bonds of love in Christ (Rom. 12.8). Along with helps, mercy, and healing, the gift of giving looks out for the tangible good of others in the community. By sharing time and resources, the gift-giver provides a concrete witness to the essential gratitude of creatures to their common Creator as well as a tangible expression of the unity of those joined by faith in Christ. 'God loves a cheerful giver' (2 Cor. 9.6) because such a person is a generous overflow of his own abundant love and grace. Appropriately twinned with hospitality, this gift expresses the sacrificially self-giving side of what also must be a thoroughly other-receiving love.

Hospitality

The gift of hospitality brings us full circle to the impulse of apostleship, which is a form of welcome that would rather be sent out and hosted by strangers than stay home and insist they forever 'come and get it' on home terms. The missional sign of Pentecost was for the gospel not to remain foreign but to be at home on every tongue. The Spirit enables us to so give of ourselves as to be vulnerable to the self-giving of others. This is the heart of missions, but is not the monopoly of missionaries. The church is where self-giving and other-receiving love find their proper home in mutual submission to Christ, and the gift of hospitality is how this expresses itself. All believers are to show hospitality (*philoxenos*) without complaint, but this is also a particular gift of the Spirit to be stewarded along with the others (1 Pet. 4.9–10). The giver of hospitality is particularly adept at making people feel they belong even before they believe. We will return to this in Chapter 10.

The letters of the New Testament do not tell us to take an inventory and categorize ourselves according to these gifts, but the people of those early churches were certainly prompted to have a look around and appreciate the fact that each would make various contributions to the community. There seems to be some value in matching up persons, gifts, and roles in the church, even if it is only for the sake of stability and development in ministry. However, it would not be wise to turn the gifts into a personality test or an industrial mechanism whereby we slot into pigeon-holes for our own self-fulfilment. The gifts are not farmed in a lab and locked away to be activated at will like superpowers. They are more like the elements that come together in molecules and chemical reactions to the enlivening of the body of Christ. The picture we get in the New Testament is more like a fulsome, overlapping mosaic than a segregation of believers into neat categories. For that reason, and in that way, it is worth the effort to try to understand what the gifts are for and to find the 'fit' God has for us, for the sake of the church and for ourselves.

1 Corinthians contains the most specific practical–theological guidance on spiritual gifts in the whole Bible. To conclude this chapter we will gather its pertinent teachings under four headings, beginning with the observation that, for all its problems,

1   *Paul told the Corinthian church that they lacked no spiritual gift* (1.7). From this
    we get the impression that the Spirit can be relied upon to give each church
    every gift it needs to do whatever the Spirit asks it to do. If that is so then we
    might pause before we presumptuously perpetuate a ministry that seems to
    no longer have the personnel it needs. Some ministries last for seasons rather
    than forever; it does not diminish them to recognize their time has come to
    morph into something else. Perhaps the Spirit has not provided because the
    Spirit has not approved. On the other hand, when we face what appears to
    be a scarcity of resources, perhaps the Spirit has provided the gifts in places
    we have not looked. Perhaps we should prompt new discernment processes
    rather than ask the usual suspects to add another ministry to their portfolio.
    Are we fostering the spiritual gifts in the body of Christ, or are we continu-
    ally cold-calling the likeliest 'Yeses' just to fill rotas in perpetuity? Might we
    be robbing people of their growth in spiritual gifts by sorting everything out
    in their stead? Might we be leaving spiritual gifts unwrapped by our unwill-
    ingness to step up to serve? 'To each is given the manifestation of the Spirit
    for the common good,' Paul says, having taught that 'it is the same God who
    activates all of them in everyone' (12.6–7).

This leads us to the observation that rather than being strictly *for the individuals*
that hold them,

2   *the spiritual gifts are given by God to the church community, through the*
    individual. That is not to say that there is no personal fulfilment involved in
    exercising them. Verse 11 reiterates that the Spirit 'allots [gifts] to each one
    individually just as the Spirit chooses,' so the church follows God in look-
    ing out for each individual uniquely. But the gifts are not primarily for self-
    fulfilment. It is not the church's job to create a ministry to match each person's
    self-realization project. This is the Spirit working for the common good, and
    this divine concern is manifest in the enlivening of persons to and in the
    tasks before them. It is sin that pits individuals and communities against each
    other; it is Christ who reconciles them. Therefore, while the spiritual gifts are
    not for the ultimate end of self-fulfilment, we must acknowledge that they *are*
    intensely personal.

This leads to the observation that, rather than being static and impersonal,

3   *the gifts of the Spirit can be layered, nurtured, cultivated, adapted, and exercised according to different seasons and circumstances.* With its humorous depiction of eyes talking to feet and hands talking to themselves, 1 Corinthians 12.14–21 gives the impression that there is a place for the members of a church body to dialogue and self-reflect about their gifts and roles in the community. When the picture widens in chapter 14.1–12, the Corinthians are taught to 'pursue love and strive for the spiritual gifts,' to be 'eager' for those gifts that most benefit others, and to 'strive to excel in them for building up the church'. No person will activate *all* the gifts, but each could exercise more than one gift at once, and should put desire and effort into learning to use them to love others and build up the church. So it is a good idea to work through the inventory of spiritual gifts and to prayerfully consider them, and to do so in conversation with a handful of others who know and love us, and who know and serve the church. In this it would be wise not to be overly scrupulous about them, but to be somewhat liberal in spotting and encouraging them out of each other. This is good to do not only at the outset of our Christian lives but also at various watershed moments and changes of season – perhaps even as regularly as the church restarts its ministries for another year. This enables us to be sensitive to the timely redirections of the Spirit towards orderly life together (14.40), and attentive to the ways we might serve in a more excellent way (12.31).

Finally, we also observe that the logic of baptism carries over into the activity of the Spirit, so that

4   *social distinctions such as race and class are not determinative of the diverse dispersal of the spiritual gifts.* 'In the one Spirit we were all baptized into one body – Jews or Greeks, slaves or free – and we were all made to drink of one Spirit' (1 Cor. 12.13). This should give us pause if we notice the ministries of the church gravitating to a certain subset of the demographic. Is that the Spirit at work or is it the norms of society? One can hardly read 1 Corinthians 12.22–26 and conclude that social assumptions about greater and lesser should hold sway in the church. Besides race and class, there is also no indication that any of the gifts are indexed to gender. Obviously it is far

easier to designate people to ministries that match their life experience, and it may not be the church's fault if the organization of society has historically lent that life experience to some kinds of people more than others. But the church does not unquestioningly settle for this – especially if it has good reason to publicly resist the social stratification of privilege. A major flaw of typical 'spiritual gifts tests' is that they rely on prior experience, based on the unspoken assumption that we will have practised and observed our gifts in good working order *first*. But what if we are given them *as we go*; as we step out in faith into a new calling? What if the gifts both disrupt our settled orders *and* propel us to reorder ourselves in love? The church should be intentional about cultivating the spiritual gifts *Christianly* rather than defaulting to cultural norms.

By the grace of God it seems that our spiritual gifts are neither totally in flux nor tattooed on our bodies for all time. The Spirit seems to want us to be able to discern and cultivate the gifts for use in our callings and contexts, and so grants a degree of constancy to the gifts in the various seasons and needs of our lives. The Spirit's giving of gifts does not cancel out the agency of the people sharing them. The Holy Spirit retains the status of ultimate giver of these gifts. They are never any one person or church's possession, but remain *graces* of the Spirit, given to us and through us to the church, and to and through the church to the world. The baseline truth is that, no matter the gift, it is to be given in love – not managed like some kind of entitlement. The priority of edification indicates that we may need to seek new gifts for new needs, perhaps serving in areas that are not our natural strength because we are putting the calling of God for the group above our own leanings. At the same time, God clearly wants to work with us rather than around us, taking into account our individuality along with the needs of the community as a whole. This charismatic view of the church has ramifications which will be explored in the next chapter through a discussion of how the spiritual gifts relate to the call of leadership specifically.

Further reflection

Make copies of the table of spiritual gifts and discuss them with one or two people who know you well. Ask them to circle the handful of gifts they see in you, and to put a question mark by those they do not. Do so yourself and then discuss it.

If any of the spiritual gift descriptions contained anything surprising, insightful or questionable, review them and follow through with further biblical investigation.

Further reading

Paul Avis, *Authority, Leadership and Conflict in the Church*. London: Mowbray, 1992, chs. 5–6.

James D. G. Dunn, *Jesus and the Spirit*. London: SCM, 1975.

Michael Green and R. Paul Stevens, *New Testament Spirituality: True Discipleship and Spiritual Maturity*. Guildford: Eagle, 1994.

Søren Kierkegaard, *Works of Love*, trans. H. Hong and E. Hong. London: HarperCollins, 2009 [1847].

Jonathan Leeman, *Political Church: The Local Assembly as Embassy of Christ's Rule*. London: Apollos, 2016.

Reggie McNeal, *A Work of Heart: Understanding How God Shapes Spiritual Leaders*. San Francisco, CA: Jossey-Bass, 2000.

M. Robert Mulholland, Jr., *Invitation to a Journey: A Road Map for Spiritual Formation*. Downers Grove, IL: InterVarsity Press, 1993.

Thomas R. Schreiner, *Spiritual Gifts: What they are and why they matter*. Nashville, TN: B&H, 2018.

Max Weber, *The Theory of Social and Economic Organization*. New York: Free Press, 1964.

9

Expectations: If Leadership is a Spiritual Gift, Which is it?

Upon review of the spiritual gifts we might understandably be tempted to suggest that this book ought to be about only one or two gifts on the list: those translated with the English word 'leadership'. We could go on to argue that the managerial gift (*proistamenos*) and the administrative gift (*kubernesis*) are the ones which organize and coordinate the others, and observe that they just so happen to be the ones most sought after and effective in our churches today. If that were the case then it might be justifiable to spend a greater amount of time studying managerial techniques and best practices. In that event it would still be incredibly important to position managerial leadership within a fulsome ecclesiology and then relate it to the rest of the spiritual gifts – otherwise how would one know what one was managing? But we would know exactly where to look for our prospective church leaders, and could focus our ministry preparation on skills training and gathering practical experience rather than burdening future leaders with years of biblical and theological study. As it happens, however, the biblical record does not make managerial or administrative gifts of leadership the exclusive identifiers of a church leader. We can see they are important (because they expressly involve the coordination of the other gifts), but that does not make their contemporary or ancient forms into definitive modes of church leadership.

In 1 Timothy 3, when the requirements for the office of church 'overseer' (*episkopes*) are listed, the gift of leadership is not as central among the prerequisites as other gifts such as hospitality and teaching. The word *proistamenos* is used to refer to the management of a household, which is something an overseer ought to do well, but is not named as the focus of church leadership. In the sense that we have been using it, leadership is a more general term that picks up its particularities from the context, goals, and mandates of the organization in view. The truth is that different churches require different kinds of leadership, and different leaders will lead in different ways according to the unique blend of their gifts and personalities with the church and its people. Church leaders thus should be identified and trained in the things of God and should then foster the managerial and administrative gifts as necessary along the way, but their office should not be *reduced* to these latter skills.

Oftentimes the kind of leader that is sought will depend on the kind of church we are: on the needs we perceive and the convictions we share about church and mission. The kind of leadership each of us expects will depend on our personalities, inclinations, experiences and needs. The more the people's expectations are mixed, the more tension will be felt before and after a leader is in place. Imagine trying to find a match for every person. There is no way a church leader will meet every person's ideals. Churches have got to select their leaders based on some other criteria than personal preference. Expectations are usually manageable if people recognize the need to learn and adapt to each other, and to a new leader. But the tensions will be felt more dramatically by those churches and leaders who have let their mismatched expectations go unnamed in the process of discernment and commissioning. Thus it is crucial to discern the fitness between gifts and callings, and between the various expectations of a church leader. This goes for the prospective leaders of a church or of a ministry within it, and so it goes in the ebb and flow of their ongoing leadership as well.

To this end it can be helpful to have a broad typology of churches (or better, an up-to-date and accurate church profile) to hold alongside a table of spiritual gifts in order to help think through the fitness of one to the other. This need not be rigid and ruthless; rather, it ought to be an aid to conversation and adaptation to the callings and giftings at stake. It helps to put some names to what we are getting ourselves into, both as leaders and as groups to be led. Then we know where our matches are and we know where we will have a thing or two to learn from each other not only as it pertains to the content of our ministries but also the ways we fit them together. There are several ways one could go about this, but in the remainder of this chapter we will explore it by placing Avery Dulles' *Models of the Church* alongside the five gifts named in Ephesians 4.11. These particular gifts – apostle, prophet, evangelist, shepherd, and teacher – have popularly been gathered under the acronym APEST and treated as representative of five basic motifs or types of church leadership. Their position in my chart of spiritual gifts (Table 2) is meant to reflect their status as centres of gravity around which other gifts seem to orbit. None of this is meant to be overly prescriptive, however. The point is to illustrate the thought exercise which lines up one's gifts and callings with the norms and expectations of a church or ministry.

In Avery Dulles' *Models of Church* (2002) he not only outlined a typology of five basic church models, but then helpfully anticipated the corresponding expectations each of those church types would have of their leadership. In what follows we will draw correlations to each of the motifs listed in Ephesians 4.11 and conclude with a few remarks about each (see Table 3). Obviously no church fits squarely in any one of Dulles' categories, and no one person can be isolated into one spiritual gift or leadership type, but the exercise can still help us to spot unnamed expectations, possible learning points, and areas of synchronicity. No such thought exercise should displace the guidance of the Spirit in bringing new leadership or church dynamics about, but could be used in the discernment of that guidance.

The first thing to observe about church 'models' and their corresponding expectations is that leadership types will tend to gravitate to churches that emphasize what they provide, but mismatches in that regard will be experienced as frustrating. For example, imagine your gifts and passions lie in the upholding of the sacraments and the fostering of fellowship (befitting models 2 and 3), but you are in a congregation that thinks of itself predominantly as a Herald (model 4). Unless there is some adaptation and recalibration of ministries and expectations you may find yourself doing a great job at what you *think* you are supposed to be doing but still somehow always being frustrated, not to mention frustrating to others. Similarly, if you are a prophet-teacher leading from pulpit and study in a church that expects a fellowship-fostering shepherd who does the bulk of the pastoral visitation and life-events, then the mismatch of expectations is probably going to cause one or the other to feel neglected. It is one thing to have your time squeezed, and another to be evaluated by criteria you did not even think you were reaching for. At least if this is named you can go about addressing it, either by having the church adapt its ministry structures to

Table 3: Church Models and APEST

Models of Church (Avery Dulles, 2002)	Corresponding Expectations	APEST (Eph. 4.11)
Church as:	Leadership is:	Spiritual gift cluster:
1 Institution *visible, true society, clear lines* (27–29)	Enacting an Office (154) *teaching, sanctifying, governing* (29–30)	Teacher-Shepherd
2 Mysterious Communion *informal community, intimacy* (39–40)	Fostering Fellowship (155) *gathering, coordinating, influencing* (50–54)	Evangelist-Shepherd
3 Sacrament *continuity, presence, reception* (56–59)	Sacred Mediating (158) *representing, upholding, presiding* (60–62)	Shepherd-Teacher
4 Herald *summons to faith, event, discussion* (74–75)	Proclaiming Word (160) *preaching, witnessing, exhorting* (68–70)	Prophet-Teacher
5 Servant *existence for others, justice, activity* (87–89)	Promoting Peace (164) *reforming, helping, mobilizing* (89–90)	Apostle-Shepherd

its leader, or by adapting yourself to your *actual* expectations. That discernment process is the kind of thing that this chapter is meant to help and encourage.

If we return our thoughts to the five motifs of Ephesians 4.11, sometimes referred to by the acronym APEST, we can reckon with the different kinds of leadership that tend to be expected in churches today. Although I do not always agree with the ways popular literature has identified these gifts, I agree that these offer a representative typology of the different leadership motifs around which churches tend to gravitate. Because these motifs are not exclusive but overlapping I have paired them according to general trends in the chart provided in Table 3. Because I think of them as the nuclei of gift-clusters rather than as isolated skills, I have placed them at the four corners and middle of Table 2. You may notice that I have paired each aspect of APEST to either the Shepherd or the Teacher role. There is room for diversity of perspective on this, but I think this is a fairly accurate depiction of trends in western Protestant churches today. Indeed there is an argument to be made for centralizing the Shepherding and Teaching gifts in communities that are defined by communication and compassion. Practically and theologically speaking an evangelist, prophet, or apostle is likely to also need to be either a shepherd or a teacher to some degree. But this is meant to be more illustratively suggestive than utterly dogmatic. The idea is to muster some general observations for the sake of further reflection. Let us return, then, to each of the five gifts mentioned in Ephesians 4.11, and give some further definition to the types of leadership that different churches might need or expect at different times.

Apostle

The picture drawn by some popular literature suggests that the Apostle is the creative entrepreneur, the motivational speaker, the sociological guru. Some apostles may of course fit that depiction, but I see no reason why this narrow caricature should displace the broader picture of apostles given in the New Testament. Apostles serve in the rooting of the gospel among a people. Jesus commissioned the first twelve apostles himself, but empowered them to send others in turn, and the sign of Pentecost made it clear that this would entail adventurous abandon to other dialects and cultures (Acts 1.8—2.13). From that first generation of apostles the gospel began to spread into unheard-of places, and the Acts of the Apostles show them to have been concerned with missional, educational, and ecumenical work. This involved not just proclamation of the gospel to the public and the powers, but also the embedded work of what we might now call church plants and theological colleges. The apostle's work is to see churches – both in the local and regional sense – planted on new soil or revived from old growth.

Far from being door-to-door salesmen who could sell proverbial refrigerators to Eskimos, apostles are secure enough in the message of Christ that they can be hosted and adopted by other cultures until it is discovered how the gospel is translated and the marks of a church are embodied in their dialects and geographies. (Indeed, an apostle among modern Eskimos would need to get past the old refrigerator-salesman joke or else risk miscommunicating and missing out completely.) Apostles may typically be missionaries, but this does not even have to mean they always leave to go elsewhere. They may get 'stuck in' for as long as it takes. Their focus is on seeing the gospel take root in a local church and empowering others to tend it from there. Apostles draw deeply from networks of support. They may attract notoriety but may just as well perform thankless tasks in obscurity for years. An apostle exists for others, mobilizing and helping people to be formed by the gospel but not simply conformed to other people. An Eskimo is not asked to become a Californian before becoming a Christian. More crucial than entrepreneurial ingenuity is the open-minded creativity and humility required to be hosted by others and to listen and learn their linguistic and cultural sensibilities. An apostle is attentive to how *others* might actively embody the marks of a church rather than inventive to colonize them with the successful sending church's culture. Apostles might plant and lead any one of Dulles' church models, but are perhaps reflected most in those churches that aim intently to be Servants.

Prophet

Dulles' model of the Herald church matches very well with the spiritual gift of Prophet. Prophets may typically be preachers or activists, but that does not have to mean that they have to be outspoken or partisan. They discern the spirits of the age and give timely words for the people, bringing the Word to bear as they help the churches hear the Spirit speak to them through and with the Scriptures. Prophets are popularly thought of as people sharing visions or prognostications, but this is a caricature of Old Testament figures and a misunderstanding of New Testament norms. Nowadays prophets may just as likely sound like a 'broken record' as have anything spontaneous or exciting to say. The exercise of the gift of prophecy involves a deep acquaintance with the Word and with the socio-economic powers of the time and place, complete with its justice systems and its injustices. They give witness to the living Word by preaching and summoning people to hear and understand and live it out. They can inhabit any leadership type, but fit the expectations of the Herald church most exactly.

Evangelists

Evangelists are typically thought of as witnesses on the street but may just as well be gifted at hospitality and regular preaching. They are apt to express core gospel motifs winsomely and communicatively with individuals and groups, and thus to lead people into faith and Christian fellowship. They do not necessarily have to be conveyors of an abridged gospel, but might best be so thoroughly engrossed in the manifold relevances and nuances of the gospel that they are ready to engage people at one of many entry points to the good news of Christ. Evangelists do not necessarily limit their ministry to non-believers or unreached people. They can also be refiners of belief, reformers or revivers of Christian faith dulled and gone astray. They may be very happy to usher people into Christian community and then to hand over to other leaders for the primary focus of maturing that communion. For this reason they could be thought of as shepherds, except that they may tend more to the fostering and gathering of a fellowship than the maintaining and upholding of it. The Evangelist-Shepherd would be a good match for the Fellowship Fosterer that Dulles imagines correlating best to the Mysterious Communion model of church.

Shepherds

When people think of 'Pastors' or 'pastoral care' they tend to be thinking of Shepherds. These church leaders are looked to especially as nurturers, visitors of the sick and lonely, and presiders of baptism and communion. They are often expected to be stable guides through the seasons of life, especially present for births, weddings, and times of death. They are likely to match well with any number of the church models, but most closely match the Sacramental type. This is the case even for non-sacramental churches, who may not believe in

Christ's physical presence in communion but who do put great stock in the representative presence of the pastor in the events of life together. Even if they are not thought of as teachers, shepherds often do a fair amount of teaching, since the words used in presiding and pastoring tend to be those which most habituate people to the thought-patterns and practices of Christian life. Since Christ is the good shepherd who cares both for the flock as a whole and for each of its sheep (John 10.1–18), in an important sense the shepherd must remember to also be one of the sheep. This pertains both to attitude and accountability structures. Pastors or shepherds are called to look out for the spiritual, moral, relational, and vocational welfare and guidance of their community, and so are in turn in need of mutual support and accountability from others. The pastoral gift is certainly not limited to official positions, but when churches have been able to afford to support only one full-time minister they have often tended towards this type, and then paired it with other gifts accordingly. No two shepherds are likely to lead exactly alike. Whatever the pastor's main way of shepherding, they will need to surround themselves with others who complement it and serve alongside it.

Teachers

Teachers are typically thought of as academic instructors, but might also be preachers or counsellors. They just keep coming back to the Scriptures, seeking to understand and communicate them to and with the church. As such they are deeply invested in the ongoing interpretive and moral life of the global histori-cal church as well as of the local church they lead. They are a bridge of sorts between the Church Universal and the Church Local, seeking the sanctification of the churches and of the persons within them, and focusing on the construc-tive practical theology that helps them continue to seek to be the true society of Christ they are called to be. They may be adept at informing perspectives, but their kind of teaching should not be reduced to the relaying of information or the broadening of knowledge and skills. They lead the church in interpreting its place in the world and its life together according to the moral and theological guidance of Word and Spirit, in conversation with tradition and broader learn-ing. There is nothing impractical about teaching doctrine or biblical interpretation. The teachers of the church give people the words and structures that enable them to engage in the constructive day-to-day process of seeking Christ and speaking truth in love. This matches well the model of church Dulles calls Institutional, but this word should not be conceived of as pejorative and impersonal. Teacher-shepherds help the systems of the church to be vitally Christian rather than bureaucratically utilitarian, overseeing the structures and thought-patterns of the church so that they will work together for the purposes of building up, unifying, and maturing the body.

There is no one-size-fits-all mould for church leadership. This should come as no surprise if, as the next chapter will explore, there is no one-size-fits-all mould for churches. One church leader might oversee a congregation of 400 people who worship all together each Sunday, and another might oversee multiple congregations spread across multiple sites whose weekend worship involves 400 people all together. How could a leader expect to operate the same way in both situations? This situational multiplicity makes it hard to prepare to meet the expectations of any given church without careful attention to oneself and to one's context in the guidance of the Spirit. With this in mind, these past two chapters have not been meant as shortcuts but enablers for further discernment. Hopefully these correlations between general church models and their associated leadership expectations and gifts will enable further reflection on the discernment of fitness for ministry in any particular situation. In this it is important to remember that one's primary gift and calling will always be paired with other gifts and will seek to align and cooperate with the particular purposes and needs of the group being led. Leadership in the church is inescapably relational and flexible, even if there is a stability and a sureness to it once one has discerned the ways the Spirit has been gifting us with particular roles and abilities. The key is to find one's place and to keep finding one's place in a gift-sharing community of Spirit-led Christians, and so be a leader in or of a church.

There are few things more frustrating for churches and their leaders than a mismatch of expectations. But there is nothing as beautiful as a mosaic of various believers bringing their gifts and callings responsively and responsibly to each other with the grace of accepted service and of sensitive receptivity, so that by the work of the Spirit all things will work together for good. When we discern whether and how to lead a church, we are looking for a fit between gifts and callings, but we are not trying to over-manage it. All of the above is meant as a tool for helping us track the Spirit in the ways the New Testament has so led us to do, not as an instrument for pre-fabricating and duplicating churches according to an overly-prescribed mechanistic model for success or for personal fulfilment. We will always be shifting and learning new modes of leadership, but this is better known than unnamed, because then there can be clearer communication in the sharing of life together.

Further reflection

Reflect on the table of church models, corresponding expectations, and gift clusters, and identify which most closely describes:

- your church;
- its leadership expectations;
- the types and gifts of the leader(s) it actually has, and;
- your own leadership gifts or inclinations.

See if you can identify both the frustrating mismatches and the beautiful fits.

Further reading

Avery Dulles, *Models of Church*. New York: Doubleday, 2002.

David Fitch, *Faithful Presence: Seven Disciplines that Shape the Church for Mission*. Downers Grove, IL: InterVarsity Press, 2016.

Gerard Mannion and Lewis S. Mudge, *The Routledge Companion to the Christian Church*. London: Routledge, 2008.

Emma Percy, *What Clergy Do: Especially When it Looks Like Nothing*. London: SPCK, 2014.

Robert E. Webber, *The Younger Evangelicals: Facing the Challenges of the New World*. Grand Rapids, MI: Baker, 2002.

William H. Willimon, *Pastor: The Theology and Practice of Ordained Ministry*. Nashville, TN: Abingdon Press, 2002.

Part 4

Meetings

10

Size: What is a Good Way to Look After Numbers?

As discussed, not only can it be frustrating to measure a job well done only by results traced in an upward trajectory on a line graph, but the church should not really even assess itself that way. A church leader needs to be able to think in terms of faithfulness with gifts and callings – and even then the only true measure is thankfully Christ's righteousness on our behalf, into which we are restored anew each day.

But surely one of the church's callings is to grow in size? By focusing so intently on faithfulness and maturity rather than number-crunching metrics of success, have I overcorrected for a mistaken motivation and reverted to an inward-focused church? This has not been my intent. My hope is to shift the focus of mission, not diminish it. So if Chapter 7 was about shifting what we mean by 'growth' in order to help us focus on being fit for purpose, then this chapter returns to the question of church size in order to reorient us for mission and ministry. I think there are indeed good reasons to look at church numbers and demographics and to take them into account. Putting the stories of Moses and David beside each other in Chapters 4 and 5 revealed that there is a time to count heads and a time not to be distracted by such things. So what is a good way to approach church size, tracking it, responding to it, and planning for it?

In this chapter we explore the relative usefulness of secular business metrics for church leadership via an analysis of one of the more popular recent contributors in this area: Jim Collins. By considering his wildly successful book *Good to Great* and also his later amendment for 'social sectors' (*Why Business Thinking is Not the Answer*), this chapter will show how the gathered wisdom of managerial effectiveness can be utilized in church leadership by running it through theological inspection and adapting or transforming it as necessary. Following this, we will look at the question of church size and, with the guidance of Alice Mann, consider the best way to look at it.

If in this book it has felt like there has been more of an emphasis on ministry than mission, on the church's inner life over its outreach, it is partly because of the place it fits in this series of studyguides, and partly because I am convinced that one of the most missional things we can do is practise Christian community in the world. Unfortunately the popular caricature of the overseas missionary and the travelling evangelist has left many with the impression that church and mission are only related in terms of resourcing and prayer. But properly understood the church is not just a resource but a witness in its own right. The late Billy Graham stands as an icon for the lone evangelist, but in that case the caricature does not exactly match the reality. Graham's own ministry was increasingly intentional about connecting evangelistic events with local churches, calling not only for their help but also prompting their readiness to receive new believers once they had received the gospel. (Incidentally, a profound but underrated impact of Billy Graham events over the years has been that it got local churches cooperating with each other missionally in ways they had not previously done. I suspect this after-effect of Graham's ministry was often as impactful as the initial adrenaline shot of evangelism.)

A crucial part of mission is to have churches that witness to the reality of the gospel, not just invitationally but as a matter of course. This is not only so that they will be proper 'receptacles' for those reached by evangelism, but also because a gospel-ordered church is *itself* a witness to Christ, even before its message has been preached in words. It is a city on a hill; a light not to be hidden.

Ministry and mission should not be in competition. There is a tension between mission and ministry that will be felt in the push and pull of time and resource allocation, but if they are in fierce competition with each other we might be getting one or the other of them slightly wrong. They are always connected, always mutually serviceable, always important to one another. As outlined in discussion of the sacraments, even what seem to be the most inward-focusing of the church's activities are fundamentally missional. Properly appreciated, baptism and communion shape the church to be radically hospitable, inside and out.

So how do we plan for effective mission without sacrificing the integrity and identity of the church as a church? It is way too easy to turn *away* from ministry towards mission and suddenly start thinking of it as a marketing campaign or a demographic-targeting social club or a well-oiled machine that marginalizes the less productive. On the other hand, how do we hold on to the integrity of church without being indifferent to those outside? It is way too easy to settle for the status quo, especially when those inside have learned a degree of stability in the faithful running of their ministries together, to the point of unconsciously obstructing newcomers from coming in and messing up a good thing. How do you tell the difference between the faithful patience of a maturely compact church and the stubborn resistance of an ingrown social club? And how do you tell if you are reaching your neighbours without some attention to attendance figures and local demographics? Perhaps there is a place for attending to church size dynamics after all.

It is not as if there is *nothing* of value to be borrowed from the leadership ideas of secular organizations and models; we must simply refuse to adopt them without theological discernment and appropriate ecclesial adaptation. The marketplace might sometimes be more like Jethro was to Moses than the Tempter was to Jesus. The problem is when the church turns into a marketplace from heeding so much advice. One by one the borrowed ideas pile up until the church has incrementally become an organization with the motivational engine of marketing and entertaining at the expense of Christian fellowship. For instance, when all is geared to effectiveness and efficiency, the unprivileged and the vulnerable tend to slip through the cracks. It is grace on Christ's part to show up with the proverbial Temple-whip before such a church is too far-gone.

Jesus' clearing of money changers from the Temple was not his only act of dismay at the distortion of God's people. Also problematic for Jesus were the religious experts who not only circumvented God's wisdom themselves but also 'hindered those who were entering' into it (Luke 11.52). The opposite of over-enthusiastically reducing the church to a market is the problem of inadvertently or inhospitably closing the church to newcomers. In such cases there does need to be a renewed attention to the people who are *not* present, and a concerted effort to figure out the cultural obstacles to their joining us. In this the corporate logics of marketing, strategy, and productivity have been immensely helpful to churches looking to improve the hospitality of their communication, the prescience of their community service, and the effectiveness of their collaboration. Churches that continually recalibrate their connection to the community will still find that they are unattractive to some, but this should be because of the scandal of the cross rather than because of the stubbornness of an ingrown and unaccommodating church culture. For all that might be said in criticism of what came of the church growth movement, it did have this going for it: it helped churches come to grips with how inhospitable they might have accidentally become. As church leadership teaching has been in persistent dialogue with the corporate world it has brought intentionality and organization to Christian ministry in ways that do seem to have done some real good, even if the gains did bring with them some errant presumptions.

An example of this double-sided phenomenon can be seen in the frequent use of Jim Collins' 2001 book *Good to Great: Why Some Companies Make the Leap and Some Don't*. In my years of pastoral ministry I heard this book cited for church leadership more than any other. Although it was a management book for a secular business audience it was picked up and employed by so many non-profits and churches that Jim Collins himself released a follow-up booklet four years later called *Good to Great and the Social Sectors: Why Business Thinking is not the Answer*. What was most fascinating about this was that I still only heard church leadership seminars refer to the first book without reference to the second. It was uncanny. Here was a business leader who sooner than a number of his church-leading readers reckoned with the fact that for-profit principles do not translate straight across from one world to the other. I do not think Collins was theologically minded to reinterpret for a robust ecclesiology, but his general adaptations can be instructive.

In *Good to Great and the Social Sectors* Jim Collins identified five issues that had to be considered if his prior work was to be adapted for 'nonbusiness' organizations:

1 'Calibrating success without business metrics' (p. 4).
2 'Getting things done within a diffuse power structure' (p. 9).
3 'Getting the right people on the bus, within social sector constraints' (p. 13).
4 'Rethinking the economic engine without a profit motive' (p. 17).
5 'Building momentum by building the brand' (p. 23).

A few of these section titles (points 1 and 4 especially) are almost self-explanatory and will be self-evidently resonant with material discussed in this studyguide. Points 2 and 3 name the difficulty of 'leading' and 'resourcing' an organiza-tion in which the people see themselves as volunteers, whose adherence to the programme you cannot necessarily *count on* in the same way as employees on an assembly line. The 'diffuse power structure' of a properly charismatic ecclesiology was discussed in Chapter 8, such that we should be able to see it not as a constraint but as a unique opportunity for the church to be uniquely the church. As such it may witness to a free market world that there are communities that run by an engine other than the prevailing economic one. Point 5 might be the least ecclesially applicable, since 'branding' is a fundamentally flawed concept for churches if it puts them in competition with one another or with businesses for people's loyalty and attention. However, even on that score we might see some benefit to thinking about how a church's external and internal communications are unavoidably going to be perceived as identity markers, and so might be treated with care in order to communicate what the church really is about as clearly and consistently as possible.

It is certainly the case that many church leadership teams have learned good planning, equipping, and mobilizing practices from the world of corporate management. Similarly, the media and entertainment industries have brought the practices of public communication to a level of precision and care it would be foolhardy for churches to ignore, if for no other reason than it would mean ignoring the language of those with whom they aim to communicate the gospel. The resources available for fine-tuning a church's internal and external communications are boundless, and while there is a limit to their appropriateness, they are often an important part of keeping a diverse and transient group of people on the same page. Resistance to corporate or secular influences might overreact to the point of denying God's ability to make good use of the structures of created human existence and relationality. At best this might be a matter of simple ignorance that things could be done and communicated better for a neglected set of neighbours. At worst, such resistance might veil a church's preference for its current privilege and power dynamics. In either case, church leaders need to be discerning rather than dismissive; communicative rather than enclaved; flexible without being fickle; and culturally aware without being co-opted. This requires theological dialogue with modern worlds of communications, management, and therapeutic arts, among other things. The therapeutic arts can be engaged without being captivated by the modern prioritization of individualistic self-fulfilment, managerial efficiencies can be gleaned without accepting the prioritization of marginalizing utilitarianism, and the communicative arts of the entertainment industry can be learned without surrendering to the short attention spans and airbrushes of consumerism.

Jim Collins saw that different social groups would need to adapt his managerial insights accordingly if they did not operate from the same premises as the
marketable companies for which he had initially written. His follow-up booklet
went part of the way to helping make those connections, even if Collins might
be the first to admit that local churches could still make their alterations more
specific. For instance, consider what happens if we count backwards through
Collins' advice and make his points more expressly ecclesiological. *Good to
Great* churches might then learn to:

5   build 'momentum' for mission by communicating and connecting it to the
    church's activities – consistently, accessibly, and clearly;
4   preach the gospel as the 'economic engine' of life together – personally and
    ecclesially, morally and politically;
3   'get people on the bus' by helping them discern gifts and callings towards the
    making of seasonal commitments to community service and ministry;
2   'get things done' by empowering others to not only fulfil their commitments
    but grow into and from them; and
1   leave 'greatness' to God in order to focus on goodness, faithfulness, and
    hospitality.

In other words, while it is important to do our best, faithful churches remain
more interested in going from *great to good*.

One can hardly blame Collins for utilizing the language of greatness to differentiate the mediocre from the standout company. Keeping the language of
'greatness' for social sector aspirations has a certain ring to it too, if we conceive
of it in the historic–moral terms of a Malala or a Martin Luther King Jr rather
than a Merrill Lynch or an Amazon. However, when Jesus was asked about
'greatness in the kingdom of heaven' he said it would take the humility of a child.
Then Jesus turned the disciples' attention to the moral accountability of a relent-
lessly merciful community of reconciliation in his name (Matt. 18.1–35). To the
question of greatness Jesus elsewhere responded that 'whoever wants to be first
must be last of all and servant of all' (Mark 9.35).

So if the numerical growth of a church is not to be a metric for judging success, a shaper of its ethos, or a dictator of its leadership practices, should we pay
it no mind whatsoever? Or is there a *good* way to think about numbers? The
above considerations should lead us to reckon with what has become a common

theme in this book, and that is the centrality of the virtue or gift of hospitality. Properly understood as the crux of self-giving *and* other-receiving love, hospitality is core to a missional and a maturing church, and so is a paradigm-driving concept for church leadership.

Hospitality is about far more than having someone over for tea. 'Hosting' may be a particular and important cultural manifestation of hospitality, but it is a shame if we reduce it to that. Such a narrow view actually lets many of us off the hook too easily – especially if we are introverted or 'culinary challenged', shall we say. One does not need to be a host or even have a home to be hospitable. Simply put, hospitality focuses on the other-receiving side of self-giving love. It is what keeps the golden rule ('do unto others as you would have them do unto you') from being an iron fist ('project onto others what you think they should have'). For good reason we have looked at the exhortations and example of Jesus and upheld self-giving love as a moral and relational ideal, but this deteriorates into mere altruism or philanthropy (or worse) if it is not coupled with the attentiveness to others that makes it *love* rather than self-projection.

Attention to *otherness* has always been an important ingredient to Christianity, but contemporary exacerbations of political and cultural differences make it particularly vital. We see this aspect of Christian life and ministry all through the teaching of Jesus and the apostles, but we will have noticed it particularly shining through the ecclesial and pastoral theology of the passages we have been focusing on so far. For instance, if we return to 1 Corinthians we see that the spiritual gifts are motivated by the paradigmatic principle of love; or, to be more specific, of *communicable* love. This is especially evident when Paul interrupts his teaching on spiritual gifts to say 'strive for the greater gifts', which are then defined according to the 'love chapter' (13.1–13) in order to show the 'more excellent way' (1 Cor. 12.31). As it explains in chapter 14:

> Since you are eager for gifts of the Spirit, try to excel in those that build up the church … Otherwise when you are praising God in the Spirit, how can someone else, who is now put in the position of an inquirer, say 'Amen' to your thanksgiving, since they do not know what you are saying? You are giving thanks well enough, but no one else is edified. I thank God that I speak in tongues more than all of you. But in the church I would rather speak five intelligible words to instruct others than ten thousand words in a tongue. (14.12–19)

In other words, the goal of a gift is to be *communicable* or *beneficial* to someone else. Do not let the *unusualness* of tongues distract from the larger point of this passage, which is to say that it is all well and good to praise God with one's spirit, but the *aspiration* of such expressions is that they might be understood and received as a blessing by others.

In other words, if there is a guiding principle for the church's ministry and mission here, it is that the gifts of God to and through the church are to be mobilized by a love that is not just self-giving but also hopes to be well-received. As such it is truly other-receiving. This goes for preaching as well as for tongues; for plans as well as for praises. We must ask ourselves how they communicate the love of Christ to the community we *have* rather than the imagined communities of our nostalgic or utopian dreams. The word that conveys this best is hospitality, at least as it is explained by Willie Jennings' *The Christian Imagination* and commentary on *Acts*, which point out that Christian love does not insist on being the host but is also willing to be hosted on another's terms, even if it means learning the language and culture of the other in order to be more truly joined in the mutual confession of Christ. Understood in this way, it is hospitality that should govern a church's attention to numbers and size; to growth and multiplicity. Paying attention to numbers is about tending to social dynamics in a way that is hospitable to *others*; to neighbours and newcomers, minorities and the marginalized.

For this reason one of the best church growth resources I have encountered is Alice Mann's 1998 *The In-Between Church: Navigating Size Transitions in Congregations*. As can be seen from the title, what is so good about this booklet is that it focuses less on *making growth happen* (as if that is possible or ideal) and more on *tending to the size dynamics* of a congregation (with the goal of being wise and hospitable). Taking it as a given that churches would rather reach and include *more* rather than *less* people, Mann rightly resists the temptation to let size determine a church's worth, or to insist that numerical increase always has to look a certain way. When churches grow in size they might decide to plant new churches, divide into multiple congregations, or expand their physical space. The point is not to *manipulate* a church's numerical growth, but to be *socially aware* about the dynamics of loving communication in groups of different sizes. Understanding these dynamics 'is critical for congregations that want to offer "holy hospitality" to the people around them', says Mann (p. 6). We need not imagine that one church size is better than another, but need to recognize that 'when organisms change significantly in size, they must also change in form' (p. 1). The basic rhythms of Christian life and the marks of a church do not change, but their cultural, physical and relational shape certainly do. If we make changes for the sake of size, it is *in service of* rather than *a departure from* the proper means and ends of the church. So if there is a census in the Old Testament that is exemplary it is the one God commanded of David rather than the one that David presumed. In this regard Mann points to the census at the outset of the book of Numbers, wherein the 'leaders needed to assess what the [wilderness] journey would require' (p. 15). Attention to church size has more to do with group dynamics and openness to others than it has to do with manufacturing growth models for the expansion of business. Whereas the latter may distort the fabric of the church's common life, the former is woven within the mandates of neighbour-love and hospitality.

The best way to show the import of Mann's work is to relay her observations. Below are my summaries of her descriptions of four church sizes and their social dynamics, followed by a discussion of the plateaus and frustrations felt between them. (Obviously specifics will differ with the variables of physical space, local culture, church stability, and so on, but Mann's estimates are generally sound and helpful. Exact numbers are less important than the attentiveness her depictions enable.) We begin with the four basic church sizes Alice Mann describes, as determined by 'average weekend worship attendance' (pp. 17–18):

1 *Family Size (3–70 people)*
   Congregations of this size are like a 'single cell organism' in that they cohere in a relational nexus that can be 'intuitively apprehended' without too much trouble. Thus by default they can tend to be rather informal about communications, relationships, identity, and change (pp. 20–1).

2 *Pastoral Size (50–200 people)*
   This congregation's relational nexus is still experienced as a unity, but it is a 'multi-cell organism' revolving around a core leader or team. Thus it helps to have more intentionality about decision-making and communication so that the church can be responsive and well connected (pp. 20–2).

3 *Programme Size (150–400 people)*
   These churches are 'group-centred' organizations comprised of 'networks of collaboration', so for the people to flourish in the marks of a church there

needs to be more careful communication and organization. They may be all together for worship, but in the day-to-day each person will not have a direct relationship with each and every other person, let alone with the leaders (pp. 22–3).

4 *Corporate Size (350–500+ people)*
Churches of this size form 'complex networks of coordination' and so must be very organized and communicative in order to 'unify a diverse and energetic community' around the 'core identity and purpose' (p. 23). If a church approaching this size has not done so already, it may have to start thinking and acting like multiple congregations in order to maintain the marks of church.

These sociological observations are sensible enough to feel like no-brainers, but it is remarkable how often they go unrecognized by the holders of a group's status quo. Whether due to nostalgia or ambition, long-time membership or recent arrival, the members of a church can be at odds with one another not only about what size they *want to be* but which one they *actually are*. This is the kind of thing churches ought to be able to name and discuss so they can be on the same page about how things are organized, and about how welcoming they are to those on the margins. A church's margins can include its neighbourhood of potential newcomers, but it can also include those already *in* the church who for one reason or another continue to fall through the cracks. This is not a fail-safe solution, but it is uncanny how often this comes down to a mismatch between imagination and reality in a church's self-awareness. For the sake of hospitality, churches often need to transition the way they do things simply in order to match their size dynamic.

Size-dynamic transitions can take place by way of numerical increase or decrease. Either way, there will be tensions experienced at the 'plateau' between church sizes about which we would be wise to take care. Mann outlines these plateaus as follows.

1 *Family/Pastoral Plateau (50–100 people)*
Congregations may hover under a hundred people because they have not realized that their 'house church' dynamic has begun to be experienced as exclusive. At this size it is inevitably difficult to share the same warmth and

intimacy as a smaller group, but when the illusion of all-togetherness is none-theless upheld it is frustrating to those on the margins. The inner core may be perplexed at this but that is because social privilege tends to be invisible to those who have it, and most painful to those who do not. By adapting to a new size dynamic the church at this plateau may *feel* like it is undermin-ing its intimacy when actually it is enabling its multiplication. There can be a sense of loss as the previous 'matriarchs and patriarchs ... lose decisive influence in the system', but the growing congregation has to 'relinquish the expectation that every event' – and every decision – 'must include the whole family' (pp. 23–4). Managed well, the gains in return include more room for diversity and opportunities for ministry, as well as more capacity for social action in the community.

In the transition from 'family' to 'pastoral' size, the leadership has to learn to function and communicate carefully in order to keep relational, pastoral, and ministerial connections alive within a more diversified organization. When a church has shrunk in size, however, often times it continues to labour under the cumbersome illusions of its former 'largesse', judging itself 'lesser' rather than coming to grips with a beautiful new identity that might be given to it by God. There can be pain in reallocating resources (and per-haps slimming down the leadership or the physical property), but this allows a church to regroup in its newfound intimacy rather than carry on with mis-placed nostalgia or ambition.

2 *Pastoral/Programme Plateau (150–200)*

When congregations hover at just under 200 worshippers per week there might be all kinds of factors involved, but what is often needed is a further diversification of ministries and leadership that manages to remain connected and communicative across the whole. Rather than overseeing every ministry, leaders need to identify and equip others to lead them. They might continue to pastor the whole congregation but spend more time *leading leaders* than in the family or pastoral-sized congregation (p. 25). The demands on physical space and financial resources tend to rise most dramatically at this transi-tion, which can be hard to accept if a church has recently bridged the family plateau relatively smoothly. It is hard to understate what a dramatic moment it can be for a church to reckon with this and prayerfully accept the challenge.

There might be a number of legitimate practical and theological reasons for churches and their leaders to prefer *not* to make the leap to a Programme Size, but there are options available besides stagnation on the one hand and a massive building programme on the other. Such churches might discern other legitimate options, such as church planting or reorganization into multiple congregations under one church banner. Churches which have *dropped* to this size-plateau may feel a 'sense of loss and grief', but should not miss the opportunity to 'refocus' by 'reshaping expectations' in a new 'consolidation of energies' (p. 26). Such consolidation may require a reverse shift in leadership thinking, back to a more direct and diversified involvement in people's lives than in the leader-of-leaders mode that a Programme Size requires. As with any transition, this might be more than the leader bargained for and thus require some soul-searching about the longevity of the role, but it is far better if this is named and discerned rather than remain vaguely frustrating for both the leader and those being led.

3   *Programme/Corporate Plateau (350–400)*

When a thumb is needed to count the hundreds, the church begins to feel organizationally and communicatively more like a corporation (even if nothing else about the church resembles one). The level of intentionality required to keep multiple layers of complex ministries connected and unified begins to resemble that of a major company. This carries demands on personnel and resources that can no longer be postponed, even if the programme-sized church was able to get away with less 'slick' operations. It is at this transition that the temptation to flashiness and efficiency can undermine the core principles of a church. But ignoring the size dynamics does not help. The point is precisely to *serve* those core principles in a new situation, rather than to divert from them. When a church moves to a corporate size it has to change in order not to change, so to speak.

'In a system as hard to turn as an ocean liner', Alice Mann explains, the leadership has to think about how they will 'keep their focus on the big questions' and simultaneously empower others 'without abdicating leadership'. In the process they will likely need to 'put in place new disciplines' to enable 'planning, conflict, and staff development', and to 'establish an excellent pattern of small group ministry through which members can connect faith with daily life' (p. 27). As at the other plateaus, this is a key time to take stock of whether such expansion is even desirable. Church planting or congregational redistribution are practically and theologically viable options, even if there are circumstances in which growth into a so-called *mega-church* might be beneficial or necessary (as appears to have been the case at least temporarily in Jerusalem after Pentecost). When a mega-church dips back down to this plateau it has to be prepared to take stock of its new situation, which might require it to 'relinquish status', 'consolidate programmes', redeploy property, or rearrange the leadership and resourcing (pp. 27–8). Just like every transition, whether up or down, this could be a beautiful opportunity. In this case, a diminished mega-church could reinvigorate local partnerships that previously tended to get swallowed in the corporate church's shadow.

One can see how the means and ends of a church may stay the same, but the self-awareness, structuring, identity, communications and leadership can all differ wildly from one size dynamic to the next. It would not be right to manipulate these dynamics for self-aggrandizing and unchurchly purposes, but to ignore them would be less than loving and hospitable. When social dynamics are left unattended they tend to default to social norms. Power clings to a prominent few, people fall through the cracks, and what the insiders think perfectly warm and clear will be experienced by others as cold and strange. Oftentimes the difference between a cohesively led church and a frustratingly confused church is down to a mismatch between expectations and reality as it relates to size dynamics. Church vision and leadership may all be well in place, but if people are working from different assumptions and preferences, comparing themselves with other churches or past glory years, then misunderstandings and frustrated expectations are likely to abound. A church leader might be doing all the right things for a church of her size but still be judged inadequate because congregational expectations match the dynamics of another size altogether. A family church might assume that being warm and inviting is all that is needed, but still remain blind to the dynamics that make regulars feel comfortable and newcomers feel uncomfortable and uninvited. In that case the gospel may counter-intuitively demand the opening up of spaces for new people to contribute rather than perennially hosting others in 'my' space. This could mean breaking up cliques to start new groups, or adjusting communication and leadership structures to accommodate new types of people. None of this is done as a growth strategy per se; it is simply a matter of social awareness, loving attention to otherness; or in other words, hospitality. Even when a church is not growing numerically, this focus on self-giving *and* other-receiving love offers an occasion for growth in maturity and health as a Christian community.

Growth in maturity and hospitality go hand-in-hand, and each requires attention not only to social dynamics but to political, economic, and geographical ones as well. For example, a church could count up its attendance, break it down into demographics, and recognize that it is sizeably tilted towards a particular group (such as an age bracket or ethnicity or economic class), but it would still face the massive question of what to do about it. On the one hand it could decide simply to try to grow in size, look at the type of people it tends to attract, and aim to amplify its reach accordingly. On the other hand, it could look at its proportional match to the demographics of its area, ask itself who it is tending *not* to reach and why, and aim to be more hospitable to the diversity of its neighbours. The two responses to the very same numbers would be markedly different, but which is more becoming the church? The answer should not be presupposed. Even if a church's demographics *are* a fair reflection of its community's, there is a further question that could be asked; namely, *should we accept these demographics or are there reasons to resist them*? For instance, if a neighbourhood has been formed by economically or racially indexed social norms, might the church have reason to bust out of them?

The answers to these questions should not be predetermined by our times, but it is remarkable how often we think our work is done once we have counted our numbers and made one or two tweaks to try to increase them. Attentive and hospitable leadership will pay attention not only to size dynamics such as have been outlined by Alice Mann, but also to 'principalities and powers' (or spiritually significant social structures) such as have been so ably detailed in the work of Walter Wink. For more on this see the 'further reading' list below, where such things can be found as Justin Lewis-Anthony's breakdown of Wink's 'powers assessment', Maggie Durran's attention to 'mission dislocation', Soong-Chan Rah's diagnosis of cultural homogeneity, or Amos Yong's heightening of sensitivity to social disability.

Having differentiated between the aims of churches and corporations, we have used the example of Jim Collins' *Good to Great* to enquire about how church leaders might make the most of exemplary business practices while remembering to translate *great to good* in the way Jesus modelled and taught. This led us to consider a *good* way to consider church growth and size, by employing the work of Alice Mann to approach these things in terms of social awareness and hospitality rather than crass assumptions about the idealism of increase. We pay attention to size dynamics not to manipulate and manage it to our own lordship, but to discern what it takes to love the neighbour and to serve one another within the flourishing marks and mission of a church. The ministry of the Word calls for careful communication, the boundary-bridging politic of sacrament calls for attention to social dynamics, and the life of mutual discipleship calls for ministries of reconciliation and cooperation rather than cliques and clubs and classes. This ministry of reconciliation extends beyond each congregation and informs the relations between churches and denominations as well. Thus whatever their size, we should hope to see churches creatively released to serve Christ in the contexts they are in, rather than forever clamouring to one-up the next church over. After all, who is to say that churches must all look the same? Maybe the spirit's work in a community will be multi-congregational rather than mega-sized. Maybe the church leaders of tomorrow will oversee many small churches that are connected in ecumenical respect and missional cooperation, rallied not around brands or buildings or celebrities, but around the unity found in Christ by the Spirit bringing people together for good.

Further reflection

Look at the five social sector issues identified by Jim Collins and at the suggestions for further adaptation to church. Pick one that strikes a chord with any of the pressures you feel or passions you have, and write down any further ideas.

Use Alice Mann's church size and plateau descriptions to reflect upon your own experience:

What size is your church?
Is it the same as what people *think* it is or *wish* it would be?
Is it the size that the current leadership *is set up for*?
How might leaders and congregation get on the same page about this?

What difference does it make to think of church size dynamics in terms of hospitality to those on the margins? Think of one thing that needs addressing in your church.

Imagine you lead a church that is at a plateau, feels called to prepare for increase, and is doing the right things to be hospitable. What would be your preferred church growth method? For each of the following list pragmatic or theological pros and cons:

Expand on the current site.
Plant a new church elsewhere.
Form multiple congregations on site.
Form satellite congregations off site.
Add worship services at other times.
Partner or merge with another church.
Revisit when you are bursting at the seams.

Further reading

Jim Collins, *Good to Great and the Social Sectors*, London: HarperCollins, 2005.

Maggie Durran, *Regenerating Local Churches*. Norwich: Canterbury Press, 2006.

Willie J. Jennings, *The Christian Imagination: Theology and the Origins of Race*. London: Yale University Press, 2010.

Willie J. Jennings, *Acts*. Louisville, KY: Westminster John Knox, 2017.

Timothy Keller, 'Leadership and Church Size Dynamics,' 2010, online at http://seniorpastorcentral.com/wp-content/uploads/2016/11/Tim-Keller-Size-Dynamics.pdf

Justin Lewis-Anthony, 'Know Who You are Set Over: Responsibility', in *If You Meet George Herbert on the Road, Kill Him*. London: Mowbray, 2009.

Alice Mann, *The In-Between Church: Navigating Size Transitions in Congregations*, www.alban.org. Durham, NC: Alban Institute, 1998.

Emma Percy, 'Weaning: The Art of Managing Change', in *What Clergy Do*. London: SPCK, 2014.

Soong-Chan Rah, *Many Colors: Cultural Intelligence for a Changing Church*. Chicago, IL: Moody, 2010.

Andrew Rumsey, *Parish: An Anglican Theology of Place*. London: SCM, 2017.

Richard Twiss, *Rescuing the Gospel from the Cowboys: A Native American Expression of the Jesus Way*. Downers Grove, IL: InterVarsity Press, 2015.

Jean Vanier, 'Growth' and 'Welcome', in *Community and Growth: Our Pilgrimage Together*. Toronto: Griffin Press, 1979.

Walter Wink, *Unmasking the Powers (Powers, vol. 2): The Invisible Forces That Determine Human Existence*. Minneapolis, MN: Augsburg Fortress, 1986.

Amos Yong, *The Bible, Disability, and the Church: A New Vision of the People of God*. Grand Rapids, MI: Eerdmans, 2011.

11

Politics: Does Jesus Inform Group Dynamics?

A studyguide cannot hope to address every practicality, but it can show how its theological convictions bear themselves out in some specific practices. As we narrow in on some practical detail, the goal is to encourage further discernment and wisdom, not to ask readers to copy and paste inattentively. These last two chapters look at one of the most inevitable and onerous aspects of church leadership: namely, meetings. In this chapter we will return to Matthew 18 in order to capture the heart of a Christian meeting, and in the final chapter we will focus particularly on our approach to those meetings where decisions are made. In the process it should become clear that our ecclesiology is reflected in our approach to meetings, even if we never thought of it all that much before. This should hopefully enable readers to revitalize their approach to meetings with some newfound intentionality and zeal.

Sometimes it seems like the most dreaded words in church are 'meetings' and 'politics'. When people say they have a church meeting it often sounds like they want to spit. When people talk about church politics it is often to explain why they do not attend anymore. Perhaps these are simply reflections of common human tensions that are not unique to the church, but there does seem to be something about church culture that can make them worse. One factor might be the fact that churches have no entrance requirements when it comes to personal maturity, social awkwardness, or vulnerability to the corruptions of power. Another factor might simply be the level of earnestness each believer brings to the cause. Opinions about matters of faith can be diverse and personal, and in the process of sharing them we can tend to be unintentionally coercive or spiritually manipulative (as in the expression *I feel God is telling us to do this*).

This heightens the feeling that those with alternative views must either fight, flee, or suppress their spirit (perhaps thinking *maybe something is wrong with me if I do not feel the same way*). Another factor might be the false idea in some church cultures that it is less spiritual to have a planned agenda to a meeting, or to converse in an orderly fashion. This oftentimes underlines a subconscious confusion of individual self-confidence with gathered Christian assurance, thus privileging those who have the force of personality or the social capital to speak up more quickly on behalf of the rest. None of these social phenomena is the monopoly of the church, but when we put these and other factors together it can feel as if whatever is bad about meetings and relational politics in general is exponentially worse in the church.

The issues we have with church politics will likely be variations on the basic human problems of communication and power, but churches can be breeding grounds for uniquely bad politics that get ground into the spiritual and social dynamics in a way that is pathological. This is doubly grievous when we consider the kind of witness this makes of a church community that is meant to be a beacon of grace and truth.

In one sense it is wrong to expect the church to be any different to any other group; after all, we are still sinners. But in another sense it is right to hope for better from communities that confess Jesus as Lord, gather to share God's grace, and endeavour to practise social dynamics wherein mercy abounds and truth can be spoken in love.

Despite the pathologies I have thus far described in all-too familiar tones, I must confess that I really value church meetings. Recently I was trying to explain to someone why I prefer the problem of three-hour meetings to the problem of no meetings at all, and it was helpful for me to hear the deep frustration this person felt in reverse. In this person's view it was much more preferable if we could make our decisions in corridors and offices, with short and sweet conversations between the people involved, rather than in a full room where everyone has to say their piece. That is certainly a fair observation, and in many cases would be an appropriately efficient way to do things. Too often there are questions that make it onto a meeting agenda that could have been less painfully dealt with elsewhere, if systems had been in place to empower leaders to answer them accountably. However, there are also questions that get decided in corridors and phone calls that ought to have been discussed practically and theologically in leadership meetings. By assuming these can be dealt with in corridors, we may effectively cut segments of the leadership out of the conversation, or ensure that some are invited too late. As a regular pattern of deliberation this will be particularly disadvantageous to those on a leadership team who do not travel the corridors looking for a dozen conversations a day, due to unavailability or personality or conviction. Unfortunately, once deliberations have snowballed in a particular direction and have taken on a life of their own, those who are a step behind will have been disempowered, perhaps illegitimately. A decision might be made which is in the end called a consensus, but some may have been more cornered into it than others. The group may claim to have arrived at a decision without any one person asserting their authority, but whoever took responsibility for moving the conversation along from room to room will inevitably have exerted more influence over the decision than others. I value meetings because some things require gathered deliberation, and because they give us a chance to overcome these hidden obstacles. Meetings can be a gift to a leadership team: a gift of time and space that the members of the group give to one another for the purpose of seeking the Lord's will together all at once.

Meetings are experienced differently by extroverts and introverts; by verbal and internal processors; by contemplatives and activists; by those with social privilege and those without. The problem some people have with meetings is that they do not feel them to be safe places to have frank and efficient conversations. Others feel the same way about corridors. Some people think and articulate themselves better in smaller, more informal conversations, and others in a more ordered and intentional format. Leadership teams need to have wisdom to know when a meeting is called for, and to make sure there is clarity among the group about when it is and how it will proceed. They also need to have the grace and respect to make room for each other so that deliberations can be safe and honest, efficient, and clear. There is something of an art to this. It takes a combined effort on the part of those who gather for a meeting and those who lead them.

Of course, if we have had bad experiences we might be excused for treating *church politics* and *meetings* as if they are four-letter words. But the answer is not to eradicate all meetings and pretend that we can be *apolitical* simply by choosing not to have them. There are always politics involved in church life and community, and this does not go away if we default into spontaneity any more than if we pre-plan every meeting to the second. Some seem to think that the way to do meetings in the fellowship of the Spirit is to take all the planning out of them. This is an understandable and sometimes timely response to oppressive rigidity or authoritarian control, but is hardly an appropriately Christian rule of thumb. There is no reason to assume the Spirit prefers spontaneity to planning in principle. Even in a chapter where he seems to be setting the stage for some fairly open and flexible meetings, Paul still concluded that 'all things should be done decently and in order' (1 Cor. 14.40). There is no such thing as a lack of order, there is only the question of how clear and accessible the order is to the group.

The meetings that try hardest to be the least politically ordered are often themselves the most apt to be *politicized*. We may rightly strive to be collaborative, but we deceive ourselves if we think that collaboration automatically excludes leadership or informality eliminates expressions of authority, even among groups of close friends. Something will inevitably come up that reveals the leader. To paraphrase the opening line of Carl Schmitt's 1922 *Political Theology*, the one in charge is the one 'who decides an exception' (p. 5). If no one wants to do *that*, then the leader is whoever decides who decides. If no one wants to do *that*, then the leader is the one who calls the meeting. On it goes. Groups may decide to assign leadership on a fluid and informal basis, but they should not pretend to have no leaders, and should be prepared to deal with higher degrees of misunderstanding about how decisions get made and things get done. Absent of roles, responsibilities, and rules of engagement of any kind, meetings will still be influenced by personal and social dynamics – some virtuous, some vicious; some visible and some under the surface; some shaped by Christian impulses and some by cultural norms. The power dynamics of such meetings are often most invisible to those who are most advantaged by them, and most visible to those whom they marginalize. We cannot avoid church politics, either in leadership meetings or in gatherings for worship. There are always social dynamics at play.

Fortunately, we need not see the inevitability of politics as a liability but as an opportunity for the church to be church. Neither the gospel nor the church is apolitical. This is not to say they are *partisan*, but they are inevitably *political*. Not only does the gospel have social *ramifications*, it has an inherently social *dimension*. Too many arguments have been had which set up a false dilemma between the social and the personal and then try to reconcile them by putting one over and against the other. While the gospel cannot be collapsed into its social dimension, neither can it be reduced to the personal. To overstate the personal at the expense of the social would itself be a reflection of modern political theory (which essentializes the autonomous individual), whether we were conscious of it or not. The truth of the gospel is that the various dimensions of our creatureliness are reconciled to God and each other in Christ. Just because this is not always our experience does not make it any less a reality and a hope we have in Jesus. Thus while the church should be careful never to align itself or the gospel with a political party, it should not let this keep it from attending to the internal and external politics of its worship, discipleship and decision making. As noted in Chapter 1, just because we shift the language from governance to leadership does not mean we have eliminated the politics. All we have actually done is shift the politic, and at worst perhaps disguise it. The answer is not to pretend to have *no* church politics, but to reach for decidedly *Christian* church politics. This applies to all of the church's activities, but is particularly potent in regard to leadership meetings.

The Bible does not detail how exactly to have a good meeting. It does, however, offer examples and teachings that can be instructive for us – some of which have already been considered in previous chapters. To get our bearings for the practical–theological exploration of meetings in the final chapter, in the remainder of this chapter we will take a few cues from Matthew 18, asking how Jesus informs our church politics.

Although Jesus' teaching in Matthew 18.15–21 is specifically about the confrontation of sin between persons, there are suggestions from the surrounding context that it may more broadly inform our approach to moral accountability (18.5–18) and to the shared intercessions (and therefore endeavours) of the church (19). In 18.20 Jesus seems to suggest that his instructions provide the basic impulses for a church's gathering. Even if the verses are most directly applicable to situations where one person has been sinned against by another, the question arises whether such situations are always so cut and dried. Does the instruction that Jesus provides also apply to those conversations that first aim to learn who exactly has sinned against who – and how? How often has something that seemed like a sin in one direction actually turned out to go both ways, or to mostly involve misunderstandings, or to be an occasion for simply working out differences? Does Jesus' instruction only kick in when it is 100 per cent clear that a sin between two people has taken place 100 per cent in one direction, or does the spirit of the teaching extend to fuzzier circumstances as well?

While I do not want to turn Jesus' specific teaching into a prescription for meetings beyond his intent, I do think it is warranted to observe a few guiding patterns in the instructions he gave. Beginning at 18.14, then, let us take it line by line and gather some insights that show how Jesus might inform our church politics.

'So it is not the will of your Father in heaven that one of these little ones should be lost' (18.14). When Jesus says that this applies to the sheep who has been part of the fold but has gone astray, it tells us that God is not content for God's people to settle into a rut without concern for those who are no longer present. Extrapolated further, this may have profound implications for the moral fabric of church life and for the situations of so-called excommunication that come up in 18.17, but there is also a simple insight here for the dynamics of a church meeting. Is everyone there who ought to be there? If not, why not? Business meetings often have rules about the quorum (or minimum amount) required before a proper meeting can be held, but this should not diminish the church's alertness to all of those who used to belong but are absent. Such non-participation should not go unnoticed or unattended for long, even if there is not necessarily any 'strayness' implied. Furthermore, taking the spirit of the parable slightly further, even if everyone is present who ought to be there, we might still be led to ask whether the dynamics of the meeting are illegitimately allowing some to apply more of a presence than others.

'If another member of the church sins against you, go and point out the fault when the two of you are alone. If the member listens to you, you have regained that one' (18.15). If this verse (and the one that follows) empowers victims with support in the pursuit of justice, it also seems to put the onus on offended parties to always be the instigators of reconciliation. But this potential imbalance of responsibility appears to be corrected by Jesus' teaching about sacrifices in Matthew 5, where we see that Jesus also instructs offending parties to seek reconciliation:

> When you are offering your gift at the altar, if you remember that your brother or sister has something against you, leave your gift there before the altar and go; first be reconciled to your brother or sister, and then come and offer your gift. (Matt. 5.23–24)

Is it too much if we extend this to apply to the offering of spiritual gifts of leadership? When applied to the context of the church's leadership meetings, verses

like these serve as standing reminders to not let interpersonal sins go unreconciled – especially between those who are commissioned to deliberate on behalf
of the whole. Sins and resentments should not be allowed to go unchecked, thus
running the risk of negatively affecting not only the health of the church but
also the dynamics of meetings. Nor should matters that could be worked out
between two persons be allowed to implicate a larger group before their time.
When interpersonal differences are allowed to influence group dynamics it has
a way of side-tracking or even sabotaging deliberations, not to mention the
well-being and peaceability of those concerned. Those accepting responsibility to meet on behalf of the church should thus accept responsibility for their
relational maturity in this regard, and those responsible for giving leadership
should encourage an ethos that fosters health rather than an environment where
sin and resentment festers.

'*But if you are not listened to, take one or two others along with you, so that every
word may be confirmed by the evidence of two or three witnesses*' (18.16). These
instructions show Jesus' preference for things to be worked out one on one,
but also show that such things are important enough to afford larger church
accountability and assistance, both for the sake of empowering and protect-
ing victims and for providing the accused a proper hearing. These instructions
also assume some degree of leadership responsibility in the church, and make
clear that such oversight is moral and relational before it is procedural and
strategic. There is a clear concern for truthful accuracy and loving discretion
in the very brief instructions Jesus gives, and these impulses should carry over
into decision-making meetings and the working out of differences just as much
as they guide matters of moral and relational discord. As for those grievous
situations of refusal, we should note that what may sound to our ears objection-
ably exclusive is filled in by Jesus' teaching with compassion and openness.

'*If the member refuses to listen to them, tell it to the church; and if the offender
refuses to listen even to the church, let such a one be to you as a Gentile and a tax
collector*' (18.17). Here we see that Jesus does not want the church that comes
to the end of an unsuccessful attempt at reconciliation to then pretend that
everything is fine. Those who have reached a stalemate over what the church
continues to believe is a matter of unrepented sin, must name that unrepent-
ance for what it is: a break in the fellowship. This break is not a result of the sin

itself, but the persistence of impenitence in the face of the church's decision. The only circumstance for exclusion from the church is the unrepentant refusal of the offender to accept the decision of the church about the sin confronted. But here is where we must be careful, because one who has broken fellowship is not for Jesus meant to become the subject of persecution. Such a person is to be treated along the lines of Jesus' own treatment of tax collectors and outsiders: which means they are to be loved and engaged with as neighbours even if not any longer as members of the fellowship. This entails an honest change of relationship and in some cases may entail a request for distance from the offended party, but it categorically does not instruct shunning or hatred. As in 18.15 and in chapter 5, Matthew is clear about Jesus' goal for the church, which is to regain fellowship with one another and to be reconciled. The freedoms of individuals are respected and allegiance is unforced, but any departure from the fellowship is lamented as a loss, not celebrated in terms of purity or the narrowing down of a remnant. We may be drifting somewhat from the implications for meetings in general, but the spirit of these instructions is relevant, and if the meeting in question is ever to involve one of these incidents where sin has been brought to the church leadership, then these verses are apropos. Jesus invests himself in such meetings, and so should we.

'*Truly I tell you, whatever you bind on earth will be bound in heaven, and whatever you loose on earth will be loosed in heaven*' (18.18). What this means is debatable. Some take it as the authorization of church leaders to make binding decisions about morality, theology, or biblical interpretation. God is so dedicated not only to the mission but to our involvement in it that our decisions at times like this are binding upon reality, for better or for worse. God's purposes will still prevail, but the form of their accomplishment will take into account what we have done, will either be with us or despite us. It is important that our confrontation of sin and working out of differences be informed by this recognition that heaven and earth are both tied up in what happens. Christians who meet should make it their mission to confess Jesus as Lord and look to the Spirit to guide them into truth together.

'*Again, truly I tell you, if two of you agree on earth about anything you ask, it will be done for you by my Father in heaven. For where two or three are gathered in my name, I am there among them*' (18.19–20). Although this has sometimes been taken out of context and applied as if God is a wish-granting genie in a bottle, we should not over-react against such a misinterpretation and miss the promise that is still there. It appears that Jesus intended to bless the efforts at reconciliation between two parties, such that when they come to agree in Jesus' name it will be honoured by God and the very presence of Christ with them will be guaranteed. There is much to hope for here. In a sense this promise is the backbone of the third mark of a church, which is church discipline, fellowship, or mutual discipleship. The promise is not that everything will be made better immediately, but that Jesus will be *among them* specifically. This could almost be afforded the sacredness of a sacrament.

This is how things get done on earth from heaven: when people come together and agree, or confess, or come to say the same thing about something, in Jesus' name. This is where Jesus is concretely present and active on the earth, even though his own resurrected body is at the right hand of God the Father. Even *before* an agreement is reached, when we have come together in his name for this ministry of reconciliation, Jesus is there among us. While the context is specifically related to issues of confronted sin between persons, by the end of Jesus' instruction we can see the implication that there is plenty more at stake than just those narrow circumstances. There is a rule of life to be traced through this which can be worked out in meetings as well. It is not worked out mechanically as if Jesus' presence and his promise are a secret code we can possess and put to work to our own devices. The promise remains a promise that is delivered on by Jesus, in process, with people. It is not ours to hurry or manipulate this process, but to pursue it faithfully and attentively, graciously and patiently. We do so by confessing Christ and speaking truth in love in the hopes that the Spirit will lead into agreement about what to believe and say and do.

'Then Peter came and said to him, "Lord, if another member of the church sins against me, how often should I forgive? As many as seven times?" Jesus said to him, "Not seven times, but, I tell you, seventy-seven times'* (18.21–22). As Peter sensed in Jesus' teaching, the implication of these churchly instructions was that the whole process would need to be seasoned with a whole lot of grace. Practically speaking, this means those who come together in Jesus' name are confessing his Lordship, sharing his forgiveness, submitting their biases and blind spots to Christ, and placing their hope with the church that God will mercifully continue to guide through Word and Spirit. Whether we are having meetings of a sensitive nature, meetings of great magnitude, or meetings to work things out in the mundane, all of them require a relentless commitment to seek God's mercy new every moment, and to do so with one another as well. This *is* the church's politic: the dynamic at the core of what a church represents to itself and to the world. Such patterns and impulses should season our decision-making meetings just as much as they govern our reconciliatory ones. The key to churchly conversation is persistent Christ-confession, and the engine of that persistence is the forgiveness given freely for all in Jesus. This gift has been given once and for all, and it continues to be given afresh each day. This is not something we accept repeatedly as individuals without extending it just the same. The manifestation of our belief in the grace of Christ is that we are freed to speak truthfully in love, depending upon the Lord to hold it all together moment to moment, even and especially when things feel like they are hanging on by a thread.

This re-engagement with Matthew 18 has picked up a number of threads that have been woven throughout this studyguide because whatever practicalities we might suggest for meetings ought to be fuelled by these guiding impulses and framed within these overarching concerns. Even if we are not discussing sins but differences, even if we are just exploring different options, these fundamentally *Christian* dynamics are meant to be at the heart of the enterprise. If they are, we will have been enjoying the real presence of the Lord Jesus Christ in our meetings well before we ever came to a decision. And if the *way* we process decisions in itself might be as much a witness to the presence of Christ as whatever is at stake in the decision itself, then our attitude to church meetings should be not only interested but hopeful.

Perhaps this all sounds a bit romanticized next to the procedural humdrum and annoyance of pesky meetings, but there is drama in the mundane if what is at stake in even the smallest decisions is the submission of God's people to God. A persistent pattern of seemingly pointless proceduralism might veil an unwillingness to face issues openly and honestly, but it can also be a sign that things are ticking along rather healthily at the moment. It is okay if meetings are boring sometimes. Not everything has be entertaining, and not everything that is exciting is good. If entertainment is what we care about we end up conforming everything to suit our insatiable desire for novelty and gratification. One look at the state of western news media today (despite the best intentions of journalists) shows how harmful this entertainment-addiction can be. If we clamour around snappy sound bites we get the politics we deserve. We should not fear due process or the boring meeting, even as we endeavour to make them useful and interesting. In every mundane moment we might be on the front lines of the ongoing ministry of Christ's reconciliation, whether we can see it at the time or not. So we had better get to work and do our best with these meetings, whether we like them or not. There are all kinds of creative ways to work a system so that meetings are snappy and interesting, productive and enjoyable, but the most important thing is that church leaders look to hold meetings that are caught up in the politics of Christ. When we approach church meetings this way, we enact a theological decision more crucial than any decisions pending on the agenda.

Further reflection

Imagine you have been asked to begin a leadership team meeting with prayer. Write a prayer that frames the meeting and asks for it to be a reflection of a Christian social dynamic, being as specific as possible about what that would look like.

Meditate on Matthew 18 as it applies to the inner life of the church, focusing on the value it places on the life and involvement of the individual, as well as the place it gives to leadership and the integrity of the group as a whole. Take note of how forgiveness is at the centre of it all, and works itself out not in the avoidance of conflict and differences, but in the discussion in grace and hope of real fellowship. Pray about a situation where this may not yet have been followed through as far as it might, and ask God for guidance on what might be a next step.

Read 2 Corinthians 5.11–6.1 and consider the ramifications of the gospel for church dynamics, particularly as it applies to the shared projects and meetings that are held.

Further reading

Jon Coutts, *A Shared Mercy: Karl Barth on Forgiveness and the Church*. Downers Grove, IL, InterVarsity Press Academic, 2016.

Elaine Enns and Ched Myers, *Ambassadors of Reconciliation II: Diverse Christian Practices of Restorative Justice and Peacemaking*. New York: Orbis, 2009.

Deborah Van Deusen Hunsinger and Theresa F. Latini, *Transforming Church Conflict: Compassionate Leadership in Action*. Louisville, KY: Westminster John Knox, 2013.

L. Gregory Jones, *Embodying Forgiveness: A Theological Analysis*. Grand Rapids, MI: Eerdmans, 1995.

Emmanuel Katangole and Chris Rice, *Reconciling All Things: A Christian Vision for Justice, Peace and Healing*. Downers Grove, IL: InterVarsity Press, 2008.

Jennifer M. McBride, 'Repentance as Political Witness,' in *Christian Political Witness*, ed. by George Kalantzis and Gregory W. Lee. Downers Grove, IL: InterVarsity Press Academic, 2014.

Ched Myers and Elaine Enns, *Ambassadors of Reconciliation 1: New Testament Reflections on Restorative Justice and Peacemaking*. New York: Orbis, 2009.

John Ortberg, *Everybody's Normal Till You Get to Know Them*. Grand Rapids, MI: Zondervan, 2003.

Francis A. Schaeffer, *True Spirituality*. Wheaton, IL: Tyndale House, 1971.

Carl Schmitt, *Political Theology: Four Chapters on the Concept of Sovereignty*, trans. G. Schwab. London: University of Chicago Press, 2005 [1922].

12

Deliberations: How Do Church Leaders Make Decisions Together?

One can learn a lot about a group by watching them deliberate over what to do. It is particularly telling when a group is not clear or consistent about the process of making decisions, or about how they tell when a decision has finally been made. As discussed already, there is no getting around the reality of leadership and authority. Someone is always exercising authority. The question is whether it has been designated to them or emerges from a more intangible, rolling dynamic. It may be quite legitimate for groups to prefer the latter to the rigidity of the former, but in that case they will still have to have some idea how they make decisions together. There is no silver-bullet process for this, and any process can be misused or abused – but that is all the more reason for church leaders to clarify *what* their process is and to ask how it reflects their convictions about the church. Having looked in Chapter 11 at the way the gospel informs church politics, in this chapter we will get more specific about leadership meetings by distinguishing between three main decision-making models and reflecting on the ramifications of each. We will conclude with a survey of some tried and true best practices for enabling a constructive, inclusive, and efficient meeting. These are not meant to be prescriptive, but illustrative of how our most vital theological convictions might inform everything from the profound to the mundane.

This is not the place to get embroiled in a detailed account of all the different governance models that are spread across the denominations of the church. Instead we will explore a basic threefold typology of decision-making systems

– informed authority, guided democracy, and consensus – so that we can be socially aware of the dynamics involved in each, and thus more wisely attuned as leaders. The following exploration may even help us to think through the different processes that are appropriate for different kinds of meetings. These should be chosen not only for pragmatic reasons related to group size and responsibility, but also for theological convictions about the essential politics of a Christian community. Each of the three basic modes of decision-making has its positives and negatives, but one of the most frustrating things within each is when there is a lack of clarity about the process that is in place. Rather than argue definitively for one decision-making model over the others, this chapter aims to promote the practical wisdom that will help church leaders be clear about what they are doing when they make decisions in the body of Christ.

In 1973 Victor Vroom and Philip Yetton published the influential *Leadership and Decision Making*, which helpfully arranged the different 'Decision Methods' according to four basic types. Decisions, they said, are either Autocratic, Consultative, Group, or Delegated. Vroom and Yetton broke these down further to distinguish (AI) decisions made by the leader *without* further information from (AII) those that require more *information from others*; (CI) decisions worked out with *input from others individually* from (CII) those that get *input from the group all together*; and (GI) decisions that are *delegated within the group* from (GII) those that are *worked out and decided together* (p. 13). Justin Lewis-Anthony's 2009 *If You Meet George Herbert on the Road* has helpfully clarified the group-type of decision further, by specifying that a decision might be reached by a (GI) democratic vote or by (GII) arrival at a consensus (p. 193). Given that Vroom and Yetton's fourth 'decision method' effectively takes things outside of the meeting at hand, in this chapter we will focus our thoughts according to the three types of method that remain.

Charles Handy's 1993 *Understanding Organizations* illustrates the difference between these methods by helping us to picture them according to the 'interaction patterns' of the 'wheel' and the 'web'. The 'wheel' has the leader at the hub interacting with each group member one on one before making the decision, which could be drawn in lines like spokes from a hub. This might be how an autocratic decision is made with information from the group (AII), and how a consultative decision is made *without* getting the group together (CI). On the other hand, the 'web' pattern has every member of the group interacting with every other member, in a manner that could be drawn in lines to form a lattice around the leader. This might be how a consultative (CII) or group (GI or GII) decision is reached *together* (CII). Handy also describes a 'circle' method, but this is just a spiralling version of the 'wheel' which has the leader propelling the discussion round and round the group until it is clear what should be done (pp. 174–5). For our purposes I will gather these insights into three basic types, which are illustrated by the adapted decision-making tree in Table 4.

While procedural variations may abound, there are three basic ways that decisions get made by a group, which I would describe as follows:

1 *Informed Authority*: The decision is made by a designated leader on informed and carefully considered advisement from the other members of the group.
2 *Guided Democracy*: The decision is made by a majority vote when there has been a discussion aiming at an agreeable result with a clear rationale.
3 *Consensus Building*: The decision is made when there is unanimous agreement about the action to be taken and at least broad agreement as to its rationale.

Before we go any further, take a few moments to reflect on a few questions about these three basic approaches to decision making:

1 To which are you accustomed?
2 To which is your church accustomed?
3 Which would you prefer to *lead*?
4 Into which would you prefer to be *led*?
5 What are the benefits of each?
6 What are the difficult dynamics unique to each?
7 Is one or the other of these more or less appropriate *for a church*?

Reflecting on these questions should help us to recognize that *how we decide* informs the *kinds of conversations we have*, whether we plan it that way or not. For instance, if a group knows it has two hours to come to a consensus, it will have a different kind of conversation than if it has two hours to achieve a majority, or two hours to inform the person authorized to decide on their behalf. In the case of consensus building, those in the minority are more likely to be found out and engaged in conversation than in the case of a democratic process, where

Table 4: Decision-making tree

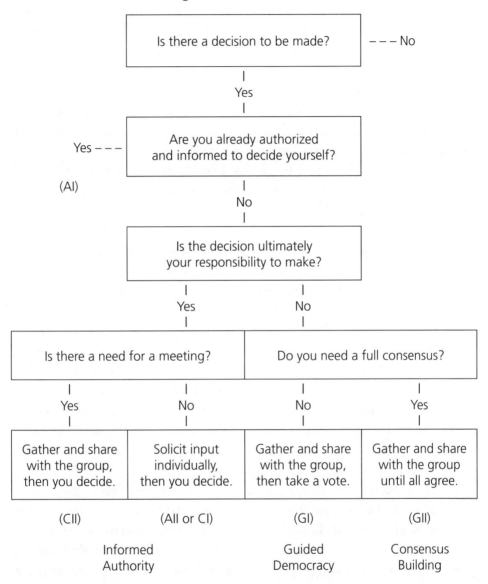

* Adapted from Vroom and Yetton's *Leadership and Decision-Making*, Justin Lewis-Anthony's *If You Meet George Herbert*, and Charles Handy's *Understanding Organizations*.
** Note: A group could vote or agree to defer the decision back to the leader, in which case it could move from GI or GII to CII. It could also inform the leader to make all such decisions accordingly in the future, thus shifting the scenario from CII to CI, AI, or AII next time.

persuasive appeals are more likely to be made towards the felt majority, or in the case of authority-informing, where each is more likely to voice their views in a manner that is geared to the person concerned. Are any of these wrong or right?

In Matthew 18.19, when Jesus said that 'if two of you agree on earth about anything you ask, it will be done for you by my Father in heaven', it seemed to place a high value on consensus between the parties concerned. Interestingly however, the steps Jesus laid out in the preceding verses appeared to suggest that, in the case of confronted sin at least, there was some warrant for not involving a wider group in the conversation until it became necessary. His instruction to bring unreconciled differences to witnesses and then to the church (18.16–17) suggests that Jesus was willing to endorse the entrustment of some responsibility and authority to a few rather than insisting everything be brought to everyone. Our review of spiritual gifts in Chapter 8 also suggested that the early church found room for the assignment of some decision-making responsibilities to some as a service to the rest. But Jesus and Paul were not necessarily laying down instructions for church meetings of every kind. Do other passages lead us to prefer one decision-making method over another?

The book of Acts reveals a variety of ways in which the first church decisions were made. We have already considered the example in Acts 6, when 'the twelve called together the whole community of the disciples' and asked them to 'select from among [them]selves seven men of good standing' for a task (6.2–3). On one hand we see an authoritative decision being made (unanimously?) by a group of twelve, but on the other hand we see that the decision itself is to further defer to 'the whole community', who were reportedly all 'pleased' with the result (5).

Later, at the council of Jerusalem in Acts 15, the apostle James claims to 'have reached a decision' (15.19) about Gentile practices on behalf of the group 'after there had been much debate' from 'the apostles and the elders' who had met (6–7). Then the group 'decided unanimously to choose representatives' (22) to send to the 'whole church' scattered across the land in order to relay what 'seemed good to the Holy Spirit and to us to impose' and not impose (28). Leaving aside the question of whether Paul and Barnabas stayed true to that instruction, and whether or not they were entrusted to make variable interpretations of it as they went, we note simply that there were at least two modes of decision making exercised within the council of Jerusalem alone. There is no mention of a democratic vote in these passages, although such political processes as we have them today had not yet been invented. We do have the category-busting example of Acts

1.12–26, however, where Judas's replacement in the group of twelve apostles is decided by prayer and the casting of lots, after two men had been proposed by the believers according to qualifications explained by Peter.

If we were looking in the New Testament for a definitive method of decision making in the church, we appear to have come up short. But neither have we been left with nothing. The early church appears to have been comfortable entrusting leaders to make some decisions on their behalf, including the decision when and how to consult the whole. A review of 1 Timothy's qualifications for bishops (or overseers), elders (or presbyters), and deacons (or servers) suggests that layered responsibilities became more formalized in some early churches as time went on (see 3.1–13, 4.14, and 5.17–22). In the early church one detects a desire to seek wide if not full congregational agreement, but full consensus is not spelled out as a universal requirement before any church can proceed. Thus there appears to be room for churches and leaders with decisions to make to first make decisions about how to decide! Since it is not the place of this studyguide to pin readers to any one church governance model, in closing we will simply consider some of the social dynamics involved in these three decision-making methods, and note some meeting procedures that have proven to be helpful tools for healthy deliberations.

Consensus Building: In my experience, many church people prefer to make decisions by consensus, whether for theological reasons or from a desire to see everyone get along. We have already seen biblical examples and teachings that affirm this impulse as a good one, even if it is not a legalistic demand. However, this is not always as straightforward as it may seem – especially to those most privileged by the social dynamics of their community's status quo. Sometimes the felt desire for an expedient arrival at consensus can become part of an unhealthy power dynamic: the perpetuator of an environment of false peace. The pressure for consensus can be so palpable that a minority voice will think twice before even daring to ask a question. We cannot be naive about the invisible balances of power on which so-called consensus can rely. If meeting dynamics and pro-cesses are such that agreement is achieved at the expense of a beleaguered or fearful minority, then a well-meaning group might unwittingly have shifted into a passive aggressive form of consensus *assertion*. The key to Christian consensus building is to define *consensus* in terms of Christ-confession (see Chapter 2), and *building* in terms of mutual edification (see Chapter 7) and hospitality (see

Chapter 10) in the fellowship of the Spirit. The goal is to agree in Jesus' name (Matt. 18.19–20), and to get there by speaking truth in love (Eph. 4.11–16).

Guided Democracy: The modern democratic method of decision making does not appear in the New Testament, but that does not make it wholly illegitimate. In a sense it is just a hybrid of the other two methods. As a form of authoritative decision making it provides a mechanism by which authority is given to 'the will of the people', however defined. As a close relative to consensus building, it incentivizes wide agreement without giving decisions over to be unnecessarily held back by the insufficiently informed or a stubborn minority. However, if the problem with consensus is that it can breed an ethos of hidden privilege and unhealthy conflict avoidance, the problem with democracy is that it can assume irreconcilable differences and give up on consensus too often and too soon. If we believe that we confess one Lord and are guided into truth by one Spirit, why do we settle so easily on democracy? Why should we be so comfortable with the democratic assumption that we will remain divided, and that consensus is unreachable or undesirable compared to the priorities of timeliness, efficiency, or majority will? Since when does Christianity assume it should favour the will and the voice of the majority? Perhaps that is often the case, but should it be *assumed*? Democracy may be the preferred way to involve as many people as possible in a decision without over-authorizing a dissenting minority or a decisive power figure, but we should not assume it is value-neutral, power-free, and infallibly inclusive. Democratic deliberations can still be de-liberating, especially when the powers-that-be are not named and confessed and accountable.

The way democratic societies have tried to overcome many of the above obstacles is by way of *representative* democracy. In a representative democracy the people recognize that it is not possible for every person to speak up for themselves about everything, so a system is devised whereby some can be chosen to represent the constituents in a smaller group setting where decisions will be made. The question how those representatives are chosen, and who or what they represent exactly, is complicated. In a church it is usually the case that the small decision-making body is not simply there to re-present the surveyed desires of the membership, but is there with the vested *responsibility* to take matters under advisement and then make a decision based on *their informed convictions*. In this way the democratic system is something of an ingenious hybrid between the all-inclusive ideal of the consensus model and the responsibility-investing ideal of the authoritative model. It can be a good system, but it does not come without its problems.

Informed Authority: Contrary to popular perception, lines of authority are not necessarily opposed to an ethos of mutual service and collaboration. Leadership structures simply designate lines of responsibility and accountability that are agreeable to the collaborators. Indeed it is common and legitimate for churches to decide (by vote or by consensus) that they will thereafter authorize some to make certain decisions on behalf of the whole. Those who are *authorized* to some level of responsibility are commissioned to serve within the parameters and purposes assigned. These can include creedal commitments, missional priorities, role designations, financial allowances, term limits, lines of account-ability, procedures for reconsideration, and so on. These become the fabric of the community's life together. Such structures can become constrictive, but by clarifying and renewing them regularly a group may also liberate itself from the tyranny of dictatorial rulership on the one hand, or from the perpetuation of manufactured unanimity on the other. They operate like the boundaries on a football pitch or the rules of an improvisational game: they free for collaboration that is neither so random that it is hard to participate, or so rigid that there is no room for the person. If authorities and parameters have not been named, it does not mean they do not exist. In any deliberation there are constraints of time and space that make it relevant to ask who or what sways a discussion towards a decision. Is it the readiness of some to speak earlier, or louder, or more often, or with more social capital, than others? There is a degree of power involved in deciding when consensus is reached, when it is time to vote, or when there is enough information to make a decision. Thus it is important for church leaders to be attentive to power dynamics, sensitive to the persons involved, and wise about how they utilize whatever decision-making systems they inhabit.

Should churches favour timely efficiency over patient deliberation, powers of persuasion over attentive prayer, or constituency-representation over theo-logical reflection? There is no one-size-fits-all resolution to these tensions and questions, but thoughtfulness about them is important. Churches should hope for consensus, but this side of the return of Christ they should be prepared not to force it, and should instead ensure appropriate means for proceeding graciously and decisively together in Christ. Ours is a time of lamentable division about many things, but this is only worsened by a hasty erasure of differences for the sake of a manufactured peace. Churches should not be indecisively beholden to an idolatrous ideal of visible unanimity, nor should they be recklessly divisive because of an indifference to unity. Instead we proceed, as we always did, in the faith that one Lord unifies us and one Spirit brings us into fellowship even *across* our visible divisions, and patient of their reconciliation. This means deploying the resources God has given to work together within our creaturely limits and sinful condition, praying for the Spirit to guide us into truth together.

As discussed in Chapter 11, a church's deliberative *process* is as much a witness to the gospel as its *result*. Sidney Lumet expressed this notion well in his 1995 book about *Making Movies:*

> We're not out for consensus here. We're out for communication. And some-times we get consensus. And that's thrilling ... I'm in charge of a community that I need desperately and that needs me just as badly. That's where the joy lies, in the shared experience. Anyone in that community can help me or hurt me. For this reason, it's vital to have ... people who can challenge you to work at your best, not in hostility but in a search for the truth. Sure, I can pull rank if a disagreement becomes unresolvable, but that's only a last resort ... the joy is in the give-and-take (pp. 16–17).

Not all meetings can or should be as openly creative as Lumet's movie sets may have been, but there is a ring of truth to the dynamic he describes. This quote comes to mind when my own agenda threatens my ability to truly *gather in Jesus' name.*

Jean Vanier puts this quite provocatively in his 1979 book *Community and Growth: Our Pilgrimage Together* when he says, 'Jesus cannot be there if people come together physically but refuse to meet each other' (p. 181). The 'cannot' in that sentence might be an overstated underestimation of the grace of God, but the point stands. Looking at it this way, Vanier goes on to describe 'the gift of meetings':

> We do not have meetings either to impose our own ideas or to defend our-selves. That sort of approach doesn't get you far in community. We meet for a very different reason – to hear each other's ideas. The aim is to discover together what has to be done, and that implies that we believe that not one of

us is more intelligent than all of us together … The foundation of all meetings is listening to the ideas of others … Different sorts of meeting have to be carefully distinguished. We shouldn't expect too much nourishment from one which has to do with administration or with, say, preparing a celebration. Community life means service and these meetings are services we render for the good of the whole. But there can still be a joy and peace in them. (pp. 181–2)

Depicting meetings as gifts of listening to each other for the sake of a shared service to the common good, Vanier preserves both the proper spirit of a meeting and the recognition that meetings are generally meant to get something done. Each type of meeting 'demands its own discipline', he says, which means agreeing to a time and an agenda, praying for the Spirit's guidance, and leading and structuring the meeting to enable participation (p. 183). But in all of this the means cannot be ultimately separated from the ends. If the goal is to witness to the peace of God in Christ, then the discourse will seek to be peaceable. This does not mean the false peace of avoided conflict and suppressed convictions; nor does it mean the imposed peace of aggressive and combative behaviour. It means the confession of the Prince of Peace in word and deed. It means seeking God's grace in the meeting itself as well as in its results.

Since the aim of this studyguide is not to make prescriptive declarations about ideal church governance models, we will simple conclude with some observations about the practicalities of leading meetings in a way that is theologically and socially aware. This will be done by highlighting some procedural tools which may feel like arcane and rigid formalities, but still be worth holding on to in spirit, even if not to the letter.

Standing orders: Also known as 'rules of order', the 'standing orders' are the procedures that are established and shared to enable a meeting to be both efficient and hospitable. They provide the group with the shared grammar – the tools, structures, and language – for having a good talk. These need not be cumbersome; they can adapt to the size and complexity of the meeting in question. Even if procedural formalities are unnecessary, a meeting may benefit from having catch phrases or repeated patterns that free people up to participate in constructive ways. To give this zero forethought is not necessarily more 'spiritual', let alone less 'structured'. Sometimes the least-planned meetings are layered with insider-language and invisible structural dynamics that are indecipherable and thus marginalizing to the uninitiated. Such language and structure may be theologically or programmatically necessary, but if so then there is all the more reason to identify such things for all involved. This makes the conversation accessible rather than obscure and patronizing. By sharing the same playbook, the leaders are empowered to lead and the participants are enabled to participate. This can be illustrated by explaining some of the tools and structures that standing orders tend to include.

Agenda: An agenda is a schedule indicating what is (and is not) up for discussion in the meeting. Minimally, an agenda is a loose guideline awaiting the group (or arrived at conversationally) on arrival. Maximally, an agenda is itemized to establish priorities and goals and to provide a plan to meet them. A good agenda enables participants to go to a meeting informed and prepared enough to hit the ground running. There is a fine line to be walked here. One does not want to provide so little detail that the trees cannot be seen in the forest, nor so much that the forest cannot be seen for the trees. A meeting that has been too sparse in its preparatory resources might be spent getting caught up rather than having the intended discussion. Either that or the meeting might carry on with some more 'in the know' than others. This does not make for a constructive process or hospitable environment. Group members may be frustrated by what feels like indifference to their full participation. Even when agendas are unnecessary formalities, leaders will still need to be adept at achieving their purpose and enabling clarity through conversational means alone.

Minutes: Minutes provide a written review of who was present and what was discussed and decided at a meeting. They record the essential details so that the group can refer back to them for follow-through and follow-up. Because the minutes are a shared record and not a personal narrative, they must be reviewed at the next meeting so as to agree upon their accuracy. It is wise to make them as brief as possible because once there is a record of the back and forth of a conversation it opens up the risk of representing some views more prominently or clearly than others, or of making people think twice about opening their mouths in the future to entertain an idea for the sake of discussion. There needs to be the freedom to think things through together without fear of being quoted verbatim or succumbing to an interpretation of events to which one did not agree. Thus the minutes should not be so lengthy as to be a transcript of the event, but not so minimal as to be unclear. Minutes are a clear confirmation of what agenda items were accomplished, what decisions were made (and succinctly why), and what actions were agreed to be done (and by whom).

Matters Arising and *Any Other Business (AOB)*: Early in a meeting the leader might ask for 'matters arising' from the previous meeting's minutes which might be picked out for clarification or further discussion. This may feel like an encumbrance, but often a small clarification at this point saves a later discussion from being unnecessarily lengthened by misunderstanding. If a 'matter arising' seems like it might involve a longer discussion than it should be given in that moment, it can be labelled an AOB or identified as part of one of the items already on the agenda for discussion. Simple tools such as these empower leaders to plan meetings without fear that they may be hijacked from the start, and also empower participants to communicate to their leaders when there are things that warrant further consideration than has been previously afforded. If a group has a pattern of lengthy AOBs it may be a sign that the leader needs to amend the agenda-setting practices, or that the group needs to be more thorough and communicative in their preparation, or both. Typically, however, these are meant as a repository for loose ends rather than a means of wrestling over control of a meeting.

Items for Information or *Discussion*: These sections of an agenda are very simple, but it is amazing how often they go wrong. Items for information are on the agenda so persons can report on things that they have been previously empowered to do. To save time in the meeting, these may be accompanied by written reports dispersed previously with the agenda. Since these items are *not* for discussion, there should only be room for clarifying questions. That does not mean that this is a chance to slip something through the accountability radar. If something controversial is reported in this part of the meeting, it should only be because it is known to be accountable through other means. If an informational item is deemed questionable by the group, usually because they have thought of something the reporting person did not, the leader of the meeting must determine whether to make it an AOB or a matter for a future agenda. Some meetings are held entirely for informative purposes, just to ensure everyone is on the same page before work continues. These are sometimes held standing up, so as to keep from settling into a longer discussion. If a meeting is meant to contain discussion, but there is no need for a decision to be made as a result, then items are labelled and prepared in such a way as to call for and enable the appropriate conversation. Sometimes these discussions arrive at decisions, but when this happens the leader and the group (and the minutes) need to be clear about it. All of this seems common sense enough on paper, but it is remarkable how easy it is to get carried away in the moment and inadvertently sabotage a meeting or disrespect the leadership. Getting carried away can be a very good sign that a group is speaking freely and comfortably with each other, but agenda items such as these provide them with tools to get back on track as needed.

Items for Decision: If there is a decision to be made in a meeting, obviously it is helpful for the people involved to be informed and empowered for deliberation. We have already discussed the different ways decisions might be made, and noted that the method may vary depending on the matter at hand. The key, however, is to be clear about this *before* the discussion is had, otherwise the participants may deliberate under false pretences about the kind of input they are being called on to contribute. In any event, what follows are some tools that help groups arrive at decisions clearly and fairly.

Motions or *Proposals*: If there is a decision to be made it is most helpful if it can be articulated in terms of a clear proposal. When someone does this, either in the agenda or during the course of deliberations, it is often said that they have 'made a motion' or asked the group to 'move' on something. This could come at the end or at the beginning of a discussion, and may not even reflect the finalized opinion of the person articulating it; the point is to make as clear as possible what it is that is up for decision. Sometimes the person who generates the idea is not the same as the person who hears the discussion and comes up with a carefully worded proposal. Calling it a 'motion' might seem needlessly jargonistic, but this enables a group to distinguish between 'thinking out loud' and making a formal proposal. At that point a line has been crossed where the group is bound to either reject the motion (thus returning to the flow of discussion), to amend it, or to approve it.

Seconding: If protocols demand that a formalized motion must then be discussed and decided one way or the other, it can be wise to puts checks and balances in place to prevent participants from using motions to hijack meetings (either intentionally or unintentionally). This is what 'seconding' is for. To 'second a motion' is to affirm that the group should consider it as such. Generally speaking, unless 'motions' have been repeatedly abused, 'seconds' should be given quite freely, and only held back when motions need to be rephrased more clearly or deferred long enough for the group to catch up. Seconding a motion is *not* a way of casting the first influential vote on the matter. Indeed, the 'seconder' may very well end up voting against it. They are just affirming it for further consideration, at which point it can then be moved to amend, reject, or accept the motion. If a motion is accepted it needs to be stated as such by the leader, usually with words such as 'so moved', or 'carried'. This obviously needs to be recorded in the minutes as well.

Voting: The way a motion gets carried depends on the decision-making method that has been set. If a vote is called for, it could be in order to find out if consensus has been reached, or in order to show the person making the decision what kind of support it has. But if it is to make a democratic decision then it is important for the group to be informed beforehand so they can vote accordingly. Before a democratic vote is taken the group needs to know what will be considered a 'winning' vote: will it be a simple majority of 50 per cent plus one, or will a larger majority be required? The group needs to know how the votes will be counted: will it be by a gesture or audible response, or will it be by a private ballot? Who will collect and count and report the votes? This should not be needlessly complex, but it does need to be clear and fair and discreet.

Action Items: The decisions made by a group do not always entail immediate actions to be carried out, but when they do it is crucial that the group identify (1) what they are, (2) who is to do them, and (3) when they are to be done (if indeed there is a deadline to be met). This needs to be recorded in the minutes and stated clearly for the group (perhaps again at the conclusion of the meeting). This may seem tiresome, but there is nothing worse than working hard to decide something, only to miscommunicate how it was meant to be done.

Point of order: If the 'standing orders' of a meeting get too complex, they might become more of a hindrance than a help. But if they are non-existent, there may not be enough 'handles' to help people grab on and get involved. In any case, the 'point of order' is a tool that gives people a chance to figure out what is going on. A person asking 'point of order' is allowed to interrupt in order to inquire from the leader about the meeting's procedures. It cannot be a sneaky way of derailing a conversation or arguing a point out of turn. It is simply a matter of procedural clarification. For example, one might say to the leader: 'point of order: are we discussing this or is it an item for information?' Other points of order might include: 'I think we could all use a moment, could we take a short break?'; or 'given the sensitive nature of this conversation, could I ensure it is off the record and confidential?'; or 'given that someone in the meeting is directly benefited by this decision, should they be dismissed from the room for a time?' As 'standing orders' are used they get less awkward and more empowering, especially if people are allowed to ask about them at any time.

Used correctly, the language of motions and points of order can be a very effective way of keeping to an agenda, holding dominant voices in check, and freeing the more cautious voices to float their ideas without fear that things snowball out of control. Those who do not like the formal trappings of the traditional language used above can find other language for it: the point is that the language be shared, and that the spirit of these rules be utilized for fruitful and hospitable meetings. It might surprise the more veteran or gregarious members of a group how much it helps some participants to have a few on-ramps into the conversation. Such mechanisms can also help leaders to facilitate good meetings without having to drastically change persona. Whatever the case, the 'rules of order' ought to inspire and not subtract from common sense, and ought to foster spiritual conversation and reconciliatory discussion rather than squeeze them out for the sake of rigid efficiency.

Whether a meeting is meant to inform authority, guide democracy, or arrive at consensus, the most important 'rules of order' are those found in passages such as we have explored in this book (and more). Above all the church is called to be a people that confess Jesus' lordship before their own, and to depend on the shared gift of God's grace to participate together in the reconciling work of Christ. Even before a church has accomplished anything, when it is operating as a church it is enjoying the practice of the presence of Christ. This in turn holds up a light to the world, even as the people of a church are a light to one another in dark times. To be a leader in such a situation is a challenging but wonderful calling. For those who are saying yes to God and taking this calling on, my prayer is the blessing towards the end of the first letter to the church of Thessalonica:

May the God of peace himself sanctify you entirely; and may your spirit and soul and body be kept sound and blameless at the coming of our Lord Jesus Christ. The one who calls you is faithful, and he will do this. (1 Thess. 5.23–24)

> ## Further reflection
>
> List a few meetings you have been involved in and try to remember some of the decisions that were made within them. Identify which of the decision methods was used in each, and note whether the group had pre-determined to use that method or just kind of ended up doing so. Reflect on how that went.
>
> Work through the seven questions listed early on in the chapter.
>
> If you can think of a decision that has to be made by a group that you lead, work through the decision-making tree in Table 4 and see what method seems to apply.
>
> Look back through each chapter and for each try to write down one theological insight, one question, one pragmatic take-away, and one book for further reading.

Further reading

Charles Handy, *Understanding Organizations*. Oxford: Oxford University Press, 1993.

Justin Lewis-Anthony, 'Know How to Make Decisions: Reckoning', in *If You Meet George Herbert on the Road, Kill Him*. London: Mowbray, 2009.

Sidney Lumet, *Making Movies*. New York: Vintage Books, 1995.

Jean Vanier, 'Meetings', in *Community and Growth: Our Pilgrimage Together*. Toronto: Griffin, 1979.

Victor H. Vroom and Phillip W. Yetton, *Leadership and Decision-Making*. Pittsburgh, PA: University of Pittsburgh, 1973.

Index of Bible References

Index of Names and Subjects